D1474132

RISING THROUGH THE RANKS

RISING THROUGH
THE RANKS

LEADERSHIP TOOLS AND TECHNIQUES
FOR LAW ENFORCEMENT

Michael Wynn

This publication is designed to provide accurate and authoritative information in regard to the subject matter covered. It is sold with the understanding that the publisher is not engaged in rendering legal, accounting, or other professional service. If legal advice or other expert assistance is required, the services of a competent professional should be sought.

© 2008 Michael Wynn

Published by Kaplan Publishing, a division of Kaplan, Inc.
1 Liberty Plaza, 24th Floor
New York, NY 10006

Printed in the United States of America

10 9 8 7 6 5 4 3 2 1

ISBN-13: 978-1-4277-9790-2

CONTENTS

PREFACE

This book is not about business. It is not about management. Therefore, there are no statistical or scientific claims of how universal these matters are. Instead, this book is about the observations of one man— me—and my decisions based on those observations.

In the months leading up to my decision to start work on this book, I spent a lot of time focusing on leadership. As a matter of fact, at the time, studying leadership was my full-time job. I knew what my thoughts and suspicions regarding leadership were, but they were all based on my own experiences. However, once I began focusing my attention on leadership, it seemed to be a topic of conversation everywhere. I couldn't open a law enforcement periodical or publication without finding an article or letter to the editor decrying a lack of leadership in law enforcement. Every time I spoke to my colleagues, my troops, or my associates from other agencies, I heard the same things.

Although it was mildly disturbing to recognize this trend, it was actually refreshing to know that not only my agency and jurisdiction were experiencing a void. Law enforcement is one giant family, and like any family, those things that benefit individual members often benefit the whole entity. Law enforcement can benefit from a renewed commitment to leadership, and it is time to get started. I know that I'm ready. When I decided to work on improving myself as a leader,

I also decided that I would do what I could to share my discoveries with others. This book is part of that sharing.

In 1995, I became a police officer in a small city in western Massachusetts. My life's journey to this point had already been very full and interesting. As a young man, I had been actively involved in the Boy Scouts. As I got older, I became involved in sports and other school activities. Upon graduating from high school, I started my college career at the U.S. Naval Academy in Annapolis, Maryland. After about a year and a half at Navy, I decided to pursue my degree and commission through other means. I transferred to Williams College and enrolled in the Marine Corps Platoon Leader's Course. While training with the Marine Corps, I suffered a career-ending injury and returned to school. I continued my involvement in athletics and campus activities. Shortly after completing my degree, I returned home and had the good fortune to be hired by my department as a civilian. I spent two years working on our community policing programs before I was offered a spot at the police academy.

Prior to becoming a police officer, an unusual phenomenon had occurred in my life. Without my being aware of it, and with absolutely no planning, nearly every organization I had ever been associated with was centered on the development and delivery of leadership. As a senior Scout, I had been selected for the Boy Scouts' Junior Leadership Training clinic. Many of my Scoutmasters and Explorer Advisors were military men who regarded leadership as a valuable life lesson. My high school mentors and advisors were all gifted leaders who shared their lessons and expected leadership to be demonstrated. The Naval Academy is perhaps one of the world's foremost leadership laboratories. Midshipmen are required to study formal leadership and emulate their leaders. They are expected to demonstrate a high degree of leadership among their peers and followers. Like the Naval

Academy, Officer Candidates School was a study in leadership. In college, I served as a team captain, a student security supervisor, and a course facilitator for a student initiated course. Studying, learning, and practicing leadership had become a theme in my life. Sometimes I succeeded, sometimes I failed, but I always sought to improve. This was a natural state for me. At this point in my life, I really believed that all successful organizations were focused on leadership.

I continued to believe that as I started my career as a police officer. Even in the police academy, leadership was recognized, encouraged, and rewarded. Student officers were placed in situations that demanded leadership, both formal and informal. Those who met the challenge were recognized by the academy, their classmates, and their new agencies. We believed that these proud new officers of today would be the police executives of tomorrow. They would continue to develop their skills, talents, and leadership abilities. Eventually, they would test, promote, and practice the leadership they were developing. Unfortunately, the reality looked very different from that vision.

Once I became a sworn officer and went to work, I was continually amazed at how little value was placed on the practice of leadership. Rather than providing leadership, supervisors appeared to be interested in maintaining the status quo. Young officers were expected to do it the way it had always been done. The attitude of the other officers was, "If it was good enough for us, it is good enough for you." Amazingly, this attitude didn't stop with the line troops. First-line supervisors and command personnel, who had succeeded in this system, expected the system to continue. The path to upper-level management was simple: you read the required books, took the required test, and waited for someone to leave the agency. Promotions rolled down through the agency, and if you were one of the top three finishers on the test, you got an interview. Unless something really foolish was said during the interview, the top finisher would get the position. As a newly promoted supervisor, you would be scheduled to attend a two-week supervisory course at one of the regional police academies. A couple of years later, you would go through the process again.

At first, I thought that the lack of leadership was about the people. The officers who elected to start up the promotional ladder were not necessarily leaders. There wasn't any prerequisite of prior leadership experience to take the test. During the interview process, leadership would probably never come up. Some of the officers had gained a reputation as "good cops." Based on that reputation, they thought they could help out by becoming bosses. Some officers had great ideas and knew that they couldn't initiate them as patrol officers; higher rank was their vehicle to change. Some of the officers knew they would make more money as a supervisor; promotion made financial sense in their lives. Some of my bosses actually were pretty good leaders. They were concerned about their people, interested in improvement and change, able to communicate effectively, and they shared their vision. They served as mentors, coaches, and teachers to their people. Unfortunately, these supervisors were not just the exception—they were actually viewed as outsiders by the administration. They didn't conform to the rest of the higher-ups and were often perceived as "rocking the boat."

Eventually, I decided to jump into this fray myself. After approximately five years as a patrol officer, I decided to take the test for sergeant. I decided to do so at that point for many reasons, but among them was the fact that I felt my agency really needed to take a hard look at leadership. That was when I found out that lack of leadership was due to a lot more than the people. As a matter of fact, at the time, what I had come to regard as leadership was being actively discarded in pursuit of "management."

A good indicator of the focus on management was the "reading list" for the state civil service promotional examination. Every couple of years, the Commonwealth of Massachusetts Human Resources Division would change or amend the reading list for the upcoming promotional exams. The list was distributed to those departments in the state that were bound by civil service requirements. It was also attached to vacancy announcements. Each test announcement would have approximately six to eight titles from which to study. All of the questions on the respective tests would be drawn from those texts and from the Massachusetts General Laws. The books obviously covered elements of the law and criminal process. They also included information on running investigations, handling crime scenes, interviewing, and a wide range of other law enforcement-related skills. During the years I was actively studying for tests, the lists contained three books dealing specifically with supervision. Their titles contained the words *Administration, Management,* and *Supervision.* None of the books dealt specifically with the practice of leadership. Each of the books did acknowledge the role of leadership in supervision. An examination of one of the texts finds one chapter specifically dealing with leadership. That chapter is 32 pages long. The book contains over 650 pages. The chapter on leadership is less than 5 percent of the book. The rest of the book deals with management issues, such as labor law, planning, budgeting, records, etc.

All of the management topics mentioned above are important and valuable. However, let's remember one important thing. I was a police officer testing to become a police sergeant. I was hoping to become a line supervisor, working in the field with my troops. Management would still be the purview of those officers above me. Leadership ought to have been my bread and butter. Yet only a small portion of my preparation time was spent studying leadership.

It only got worse when I actually made rank. Just prior to assuming my new rank, my department sent a colleague and me to a two-week Basic Police Supervisor school. This school or one like it is required by state regulation for all newly promoted supervisors. During the program, we attended nearly 80 hours of instruction. We studied everything from suicide awareness and prevention to legal updates to domestic violence policies. Not one instructor ever mentioned the word *leadership*. The entire program was dedicated to the concept of teaching new supervisors to avoid and mitigate risk. This was a thorough course on liability but had nothing to do with leadership.

After completing this course, I realized that the entire promotional system I was working within was focused on the science of management. Newly promoted supervisors returned to work and were expected to manage, not lead. We were trained to value efficiency, to practice risk avoidance, and to produce programs. The vanguards of our success were lack of liability, uniformity, and conformity. We placed no value on the art of leadership. We did not reward risk taking, creativity, vision, or personal development. As an agency, we were being managed to death, and it was starting to show. Both the officers and the agency were suffering for it. Unfortunately, I had no idea what to do about it.

In the summer of 2003, I received another unique opportunity. I was selected to serve a year-long tour as a Leadership Fellow at the Drug Enforcement Administration's (DEA) Training Academy in Quantico, Virginia. As a Leadership Fellow, I was assigned to the DEA Leadership Development Unit. I assisted the special agents in the unit deliver some distinctive leadership programs and undertook staff assignments on behalf of the Academy's command personnel. More importantly, however, I was expected and encouraged to attend a wide variety of leadership and executive development programs. I was also expected to study and research leadership-related topics. Finally, I was encouraged to try my hand at writing. During the early months of my tenure, I attended a one-day workshop in Chicago taught by Dr. Ken Brown of the University of Michigan. Dr. Brown made a statement during his presentation that struck a particular chord with me. According to Dr. Brown, the management styles of most government organizations are about 30 years behind the conventional businesses models. By implication, the management styles and philosophies that law enforcement is developing and teaching today were implemented, used, and discarded by successful businesses in the early to mid-1970s.

That statement by Dr. Brown, and several other realizations that I made at Quantico, eventually gave rise to this book. You don't have to dedicate a year of your life to the study of leadership to share these realizations. Take a trip to your local bookstore. Walk around. Find the section that contains books on management or business. Take a look at how many titles contain the word *leadership*. Walk over to the biographies. Do the same thing. It becomes fairly obvious that leadership is big business. It is valued somewhere. Why not in law enforcement? In October 2003, I took my third promotional exam. The reading list was essentially the same as that for the first two. All of the supervision-specific books focused on management or administration—30 years too late.

INTRODUCTION

Why leadership? As a new supervisor, what is it about leadership that I should find appealing and valuable? If yesterday you were a patrol officer working alongside your friends and colleagues and today you are a newly promoted corporal, sergeant, or some other rank, how are you going to make this work? What do you need to bring to the table to become a successful leader? If your department doesn't provide leadership training—and many of them don't—how are you going to lead?

The bottom line is this: As a new supervisor, you will be expected to undertake tasks on behalf of your agency and see them through to completion. Some of these tasks will be short-term and operational. Some will be longer-term, administrative matters. However, they will all have one thing in common: the tool or resource that you will rely on to see these tasks through will be your people.

If, as a supervisor, you adopt a management stance rather than a leadership stance, you run the risk of treating your people like expendable assets. This may work fine in the short term, but eventually, you will lose their loyalty and their discretionary effort. The only authority you will have over them is the fear of discipline. On the other hand, if you adopt a leadership style of supervision, your people will work wonders to help you succeed. They will want to succeed for you. The reason for this is simple: leaders focus on their people.

The U.S. Marine Corps teaches new officers that a small-unit commander's primary responsibility is the welfare of his troops. This directive sometimes causes confusion, because it is understood that the first responsibility of all Marines is to accomplish the given mission. However, the Marine Corps recognizes something profound: the means to accomplish the mission are the troops, and without them, nothing is possible. Therefore, the squad leader, platoon commander, or company commander must make every effort to take care of her troops.

Colonel Danny McKnight expresses this idea a little more simply. Colonel McKnight was the commander of the ground forces convoy in Somalia during the incident that became immortalized in the film *Blackhawk Down*. In leadership presentations that Col. McKnight delivers for the Drug Enforcement Administration and other groups, he says, "You can't take care of the mission successfully without taking care of the people. You can't take care of the people if you don't take care of the mission. Those two go hand in hand."[1]

Any journey toward improved leadership must begin with a firm understanding of what leadership is. What exactly is this behavior called leadership? What are the characteristics or components that make it up? Is leadership the same for everyone who practices it? Is it the same for everyone whom it is practiced on? These are a few of the questions that need to be answered during the study of leadership.

Our journey will begin with an examination of the difference between management and leadership. Both of these activities are important. They are not mutually exclusive. However, they are also not mutually supportive. Each is a separate function of interpersonal relations, and each must be handled in particular ways. We will discover that quality management cannot occur without effective leadership and that leadership without management may falter due to lack of resources.

Our next topic of study will be the concept of "followership." It is important to realize that there are no leaders without followers and that most of us spend much more time serving as followers than we ever do as leaders. Followership is the recognition of the fact that effective followers are not static. They do not sit back and wait to be led. They interact in such a way as to enhance the outcomes for the organization and all of the individuals involved.

After discussing followership, we will look at some common qualities of effective leaders. Although there is no one definition of a leader, effective leaders appear to share some character traits. By identifying these qualities and describing them, prospective leaders can learn something about what has made other leaders effective.

Next, we will take a look at the process of development that should accompany the study of leadership. Leadership is a learned behavior. Essentially, leadership must be studied to "learn" it, then implemented to change behavior. Both the study of leadership and the gradual steps of implementation are part of a process of personal development. The topics of study during this process can be defined as separate sets of skills. Among the most important skills for prospective leaders are technical skills, interpersonal skills, program skills, political skills, visionary skills, and staff skills. We will examine each of these skill sets.

One of the most valuable roles performed by any leader is the formation of vision. Effective leaders create a vision for their organization and communicate that vision to their people. Having a workable vision and obtaining buy-in to that vision from the affected personnel is one of the marks of a great leader. The importance of vision cannot be overstated.

Another hallmark of effective leaders is an understanding of risk. Risk is not necessarily a bad thing. As a matter of fact, some element of risk is essential for productive growth and change. Whereas managers tend to avoid risk, leaders seek to manage risk. They understand that calculated risks can be beneficial and productive.

After taking a look at the general idea of risk management, we will look specifically at one type of risk: conflict. The task of managing this particular risk is referred to as conflict resolution. Unfortunately for most of us, many organizations seek to avoid conflict. This is tragic, because conflict is the cause of much creativity and change. Rather than discuss how to avoid conflict, we will discuss how to resolve it constructively.

Directly related to the concept of risk is the concept of change. Most of us are put off by change. Change is frightening, and dealing with it requires a high level of confidence and self-esteem. Effective leaders recognize that change is not just desirable, it is essential to the continued growth and improvement of an organization. Simply put, organizations that fail to change are destined to fail.

Having considered all of the above elements of leadership, we will examine their effects on traditional, top-down leadership. Normally, leadership automatically connotes a top-down approach. Leadership is the interaction between leaders and those subordinate to them. We will look at how growing or improving as a leader can facilitate this interaction.

After examining top-down leadership, we will revisit the concept of followership and examine the effects of improved leadership on "leadership up." We will explore how effective leaders lead not only their followers but also their superiors—advocating for change, providing direction, and facilitating communication between the ranks. Leading up is perhaps one of the most difficult challenges facing leaders, but it is critically important.

Having taken a hard look at leadership in general, we will next examine some of the challenges facing leaders today, such as dealing with employees from a wide variety of backgrounds and generations, turning failures into successes, and more. Leadership is not a static skill, and recognizing that the environment we work in and the people we work with are changing is critical to effective leadership.

Once we have taken a serious look at the art of leadership, we will return to examine the science of management. Where does management fit into the equation? Does effective leadership negate the need for management? Or can the two complement each other to make the whole organization more effective? If so, where does each belong, both organizationally and chronologically? How do they relate to one another?

Finally, after having examined the concepts, we'll take an opportunity to examine how these lessons affect us. We'll conclude by examining our own personal commitment to leadership and looking at how we can continue to improve. We'll examine some of the tools that effective leaders have used to develop their leadership styles and experiment with some that can help us.

Effective leadership is not a destination. Instead, it is a journey. The goal of this book is to help each of us be a little more comfortable in starting that journey. Contemporary law enforcement begs for skillful and courageous leaders. Each of us who are passionate about the future of our chosen craft should be prepared to answer its call. *Rising Through the Ranks: Leadership Tools and Techniques for Law Enforcement* is a small step toward that preparation.

Any discussion of leaders and followers, or managers and employees, will require the use of certain terminology. At certain points during this journey, I will refer to followers as "subordinates." I do this simply to indicate that in a written organization chart, these workers will appear at a level below that particular supervisor. I do not intend to imply that these employees are subordinate to us in abilities, skills, importance, or any other means. As we will soon see, each of these "subordinates" is important to our mission and without them, we are not in fact leaders. Whether we refer to them as subordinates, workers, employees, troops, or another phrase, they are the reason we are there. If not for them, we as leaders would not be needed.

CHAPTER 1

MANAGEMENT VERSUS LEADERSHIP: WHAT IS THE ESSENTIAL DIFFERENCE?

Leadership is the art of accomplishing more than the science of management says is possible.[2]

—General Colin Powell
  Chairman (Ret.) Joint Chiefs of Staff and former U.S. Secretary of State

Like management, leadership is a learned behavior. However, where management is about the systems and the programs, leadership is about the people. Management is about *efficiency*. Leadership is about *effectiveness*. Unfortunately for most of us in American law enforcement, we're dealing with a system that recognizes and rewards management. That may be fine in the short run, but eventually that bottom-line focus will be found wanting. In his highly acclaimed book *The 7 Hab-*

its of Highly Effective People, Stephen Covey describes the leadership/
management conflict this way:

> Efficient management without effective leadership is, as one individ-
> ual has phrased it, "like straightening deck chairs on the *Titanic.*"
> No management success can compensate for failure in leadership.
> But leadership is hard because we're often caught in a management
> paradigm.[3]

Since management and leadership appear to have some elements
in common, the differences are often difficult to grasp. Both management and leadership are about providing direction. Both involve the
supervision of workers. So what is the difference? Essentially, it is a
matter of scale. One of the best descriptions I've come across is also
offered by Covey. In an attempt to provide a memorable explanation
of the difference between leadership and management, he gives us
the following parable:

> You can quickly grasp the important difference between the two
> if you envision a group of producers cutting their way through the
> jungle with machetes. They're the producers, the problem solvers.
> They're cutting through the undergrowth, clearing it out.
>
> The managers are behind them, sharpening their machetes, writ-
> ing policy and procedure manuals, holding muscle development pro-
> grams, bringing in improved technologies and setting up working
> schedules and compensation programs for machete wielders.
>
> The leader is the one who climbs the tallest tree, surveys the en-
> tire situation and yells, "Wrong jungle!"
>
> But how do the busy, efficient producers and managers often
> respond? "Shut up! We're making progress."[4]

Covey's managers' concept of progress illustrates the focus of
the management model. Management is about measurable progress
toward a known goal: more profit, higher stats, less crime, fewer com-

plaints, etc. As stated above, it is all about efficiency. Managers are concerned with "How do we do more with less?" Management is about the organization's bottom line. Law enforcement administration textbooks often refer to the administrative acronym POSDCORB. This model of management theory, developed by Gulick and Urwick in the mid-1930s, stands for Planning, Organizing, Staffing, Directing, Coordinating, Reporting, and Budgeting. Recalling Dr. Ken Brown's statement from the Preface, this nearly 70-year-old management model is still regarded as the state of the art by many law enforcement organizations.

The POSDCORB model remains very useful. It is a simple and effective way of categorizing management concerns. However, it ignores the leadership paradigm. All seven of the components in POSDCORB are management concerns. Not one of them is solely a function of leadership. Referring to the jungle parable, Covey states,

> Effectiveness—often survival—does not depend solely on how much effort we expend, but on whether or not the effort we expend is in the right jungle. And the metamorphosis taking place in most every industry and profession demands leadership first and management second.[5]

In other words, the best-managed department in the world cannot succeed if it is making progress in the wrong direction. Proper management will ensure that the day-to-day goals and objectives are being accomplished. However, if those goals and objectives do not serve to support the long-term mission of the organization, then that progress is being made in the "wrong jungle." It is the role of leaders to define the right jungle. It is their job to determine the overall organizational mission.

If management is about the bottom line, then leadership is about the big picture. Once again, management is about efficiency, while leadership is about effectiveness. If the management question is "How do we do more with less?" the leadership question is "What do we want to do?" Leadership is about vision. Leaders ask the tough questions. Where do we want to be in five years? In ten? How do I want my people to be perceived? How can we improve our organization?

Once we understand that management and leadership are different, we need to decide how they interact. Where must our focus lie? Covey provides another excellent description to show how these two elements interact:

> Management is a bottom line focus: How can I best accomplish certain things? Leadership deals with the top line: What are the things I want to accomplish? In the words of both Peter Drucker and Warren Bennis, "Management is doing things right; leadership is doing the right things." Management is efficiency in climbing the ladder of success; leadership determines whether the ladder is leaning against the right wall.[6]

An organization can be efficiently managed and still be under-led. This frequently occurs when the organization's "leaders" have "come up," or been trained under a management model. These agencies will focus intense efforts on planning, budgeting, documenting, and organizing. When an internal crisis emerges, their response will often be to alter the organizational structure, issue a new policy, or implement a new reporting requirement. These are systemic fixes to a perceived problem. Each of these management responses may be effective in the short term. The new system may encourage personnel to alter a particular behavior or to adopt a new behavior. However, once the novelty of the new system wears off, the behavior may regress. Often, the incentive to perform the new behavior may simply be that the new system is such a drag that people will do anything to avoid the requirement.

What does each of these responses fail to consider? Each fails to recognize that the common denominator in any organizational problem is the organization's people. Rather than addressing problems with regard to personnel, managers address problems in terms of the system. By adopting an organization-wide change, managers seek to solve the problem by changing organizational conditions that exert external influence on their staff. However, the employees' internal motivations remain the same. The result of these managerial fixes is often very negative.

An example from my agency will illustrate painfully the differences between a management-based and a leadership-based response to an internal crisis.

• • • • • • •

Several years ago, my agency was experiencing relatively serious problems with our communications center. Over a period of many years, the "comm" had undergone some pretty serious changes. Two separate public safety staffs (police and fire) had been combined. They had been moved from a remote location into police headquarters. As a cost-saving measure, the staffs had been civilianized. Eventually, a new communications facility was built within police headquarters. The new facility was located in a remote part of the building and staffed solely by civilian dispatchers. Newly hired dispatchers received minimal training. Once trained, they were placed in the comm with the other dispatchers. The entire facility was undersupervised.

Eventually, this progression of systemic failures led to the development of some substantial personnel problems. Civilian complaints against dispatchers increased, as did officer dissatisfaction with the comm center. Something had to change, and it had to change quickly, before somebody got hurt. An examination of the communications center led to some obvious realizations. The entire history of the facility had contributed to the current crisis, but it had been aggravated by a small number of longtime employees. These employees had been through nearly all of the systemwide changes. Each change or move had been accompanied by administrative promises of improvement, but all of these improvements had failed to materialize. The communications center was being managed, but its personnel were not being led.

The longtime employees were bitter and they were angry. As a result, they were sabotaging the comm's effectiveness. Not only were they contaminating the mind-set of new dispatchers who joined the group, but they were practicing "malicious obedience." They were doing exactly what was minimally required of them. They offered no discretionary services and took no initiative. Eventually, it got to the point where the dispatcher sitting at the fire console would refuse to answer calls on the police line. The system was clearly broken.

It was obvious that some changes had to be made, but what would those changes be? Continued examination revealed that management-initiated systemic changes had contributed to this problem. However, the actual mechanism of the problem did not have to do with the system. The system was a factor, but the problem was a small number of disgruntled employees. This was a people issue.

One suggested response was leadership-driven. All of the dispatchers would receive additional training. The training would include technical skills regarding telecommunications and computer equipment. It would also include interpersonal skills focusing on customer service, call taking, and anticipating officers' questions. Since all of the dispatchers would receive the same training, they could all be expected to perform the same tasks. They would be informed of the expectations the department placed on them. Finally, they would be held account-able for meeting and exceeding those expectations. The disgruntled employees would probably continue to buck the system, but account-ability would allow those individuals to be dealt with. By focusing our efforts on the people, we could then deal with the individuals whose behavior was challenging.

The department had been working under a management model for a long time. As a result, the leadership-driven approach was not well received. Instead, the administration struck on a management-driven, systems approach. First, they ordered that the comm would be moved within the building. They moved it from its out of the way location right into the middle of the front desk area. The expense associated with this move was significant. Everybody walking into our headquarters could see and hear the activities taking place in the com-munications room. Second, they ordered the on-duty shift supervisor to remain in the comm throughout the shift. The on-duty sergeant could leave the comm only in the event of an extreme emergency. The sergeant would then be responsible for supervising the dispatch-ers. This systemwide approach would address the issue of the comm center's being undersupervised.

Instead of focusing our efforts on the few problem employees, we chose to focus on the entire communications system. As a result, the law of unintended consequences reared its head and bit us. Opera-tionally, radio communication suffered greatly. Since the dispatchers were now staffing the desk area, something else was always going on around them. They were frequently distracted, and the level of back-ground noise in radio transmissions increased. The problem employ-ees became more disgruntled by this new move. They resented the constant presence of a sergeant. Unfortunately, so did those dispatch employees who had been performing well. They knew that they had not done anything wrong and felt they were being unjustly "pun-ished." The impact on the sergeants was devastating. They deter-mined, perhaps incorrectly, that they had done nothing to contribute to this problem, but now they were being held responsible for the solution. That perception was damaging enough, but the practical effects were worse. Some of these sergeants had joined the department after the switch to civilian dispatchers. They had never worked in the communications center. Essentially, they were being ordered to oversee a function about which they had no working knowledge. Additionally, it was not uncommon for there to be only one sergeant on duty. That sergeant would be tied to the station, overseeing two or three dispatchers. Meanwhile, out on the roads, five to eight patrol officers were completely unsupervised.

If the end result of this episode had been the successful resolution of the communications crisis, maybe this story would be unremarkable. Unfortunately, that wasn't the case. While the administration focused on managing the system, they completely ignored the personnel aspect. The sergeants were given responsibility for the communications center, but they were not given direct authority over the dispatchers. They could document problems and try to train the staff on solving them, but they did not have the authority to discipline directly any of the communications personnel. As a result, the problem employees continued to be problem employees, and all of the problems mentioned above were added to the equation.

Had we decided to find a leadership-based solution to the problem and focused on the people, this situation would have been minor. The dispatch personnel would have been trained, coached, and developed as employees. They would have been given some measure of responsibility for their own performance. Maybe the problem employees would have been disciplined or dismissed. Instead, we chose a management approach, focusing on the system. As a result, not only did we fail to solve the initial problem, but we created a whole new batch of problems. The damage to the entire department's morale was devastating. We're still feeling the effects today.

• • • • • • •

Leadership is not easy, but it is essential. Management without effective leadership leads to the kind of decisions that were made in the communications center episode. The value of leadership has not al-ways been apparent. For many years, business, industry, and government focused on management principles. In *The Will to Lead* by Neil H. Snyder and Angela P. Clontz, the authors state,

> For more than 45 years, leaders in businesses throughout the United States have been unwilling to do their jobs despite increasing competitive pressure from foreign firms. They have been too content and too anxious to hold onto their positions to make the hard choices that will determine the ability to compete effectively in the next century.[7]

Not long ago, a decision was made to address the communications problem again. The solution again involved a systemwide approach. After examining several of the issues involved, the communications center was moved again. At considerable expense, it was moved into another remote and secure area within the station. This time, however, the move included some leadership-focused improvements. Staffing levels in the communications room were increased, and newly hired dispatchers received a higher level of basic training. Veteran dispatchers requested and received advanced training. The facility received a major equipment upgrade. The situation is far from resolved, but it is getting better.

Although it is often difficult for government employees to see the value of business models for our way of doing things, we need remember that our management models follow the lead of the business community. If we are going to make the change eventually but could realize benefits from the change now, what are we waiting for? Snyder and Clontz's important lesson has nothing to do with business competition. It is that leaders must be willing to "do their jobs" and "make the hard choices." Simply put, leaders must choose to lead.

Another episode from the very beginning of my career illustrates the clear differences between managers and leaders. Although the incident was minor, I never forgot the absolute disbelief I felt at the time. I would see similarly absurd occurrences time and time again as my career progressed.

• • • • • • •

In the state I work in, students enrolled in a basic recruit training program are not considered sworn officers. In fact, by law, they are described as Student Officers. Student Officers do not have any police powers and are prohibited from taking enforcement action while enrolled in the Academy. Even Student Officers who were previously employed as part-timers or reserves lose their law enforcement status when they enroll in the full-time academy. The laws are intended to avoid conflicts of interest and to allow student officers to devote all of their attention to their studies. Under ordinary circumstances, these rules make a lot of sense, but not all circumstances are ordinary.

Several months into my academy training, two classmates from my agency and I were traveling home from a late-night class. We'd had defensive tactics (DT) class all evening and had been dismissed around 9:00 PM. Since we were taking DT, we were dressed in athletic gear and were carrying our duty belts, complete with plastic training weapons, inert pepper spray, handcuffs, and batons. As we left the academy, snow was falling. There were already several inches on the ground, and we had a drive of over an hour before we would get home. I climbed into the back seat of the cruiser, pulled my jacket over my shoulders, and went to sleep.

I woke up to find that we were just entering our hometown. I started gathering my gear so I could make a quick escape and get some sleep. We had to be back at the Academy at 7:00 AM. As I was grabbing my belt and my bag, we turned off of the main road and started heading to my apartment. We were talking about our plans for the next morning when our attention was drawn to a person exiting an alley from behind a church. This person was carrying a television, and as we saw him, he pitched it into a nearby snow bank, turned back into the alley, and started running.

Although it probably wasn't the wisest decision that we could have made, the front passenger and I popped the doors, jumped out of the cruiser, and took off in pursuit. Remember, among the three of us, we had no actual weapons and three pairs of handcuffs. We chased him back through the alley and split up to go around a nearby bank building. When I saw that he was turning back toward my partner, I started yelling verbal commands at the suspect. To my complete and utter amazement, he stopped. I ordered him into a handcuffing position and wondered what the hell I was going to do next. My partner arrived and handed me a pair of cuffs. I cuffed him up and tried to come up with a plan. Our other classmate had driven around the block and came down the driveway toward us. Since we hadn't been trained on our agency's radio protocols, he had used his cell phone to call for help. We could hear sirens heading toward us. Working patrol units and detectives flooded the area. A pat-down of our suspect showed that he was carrying tools and the remote to the television. A quick area search showed that the television had come from one of the nearby churches and that entry had been forced through a basement window. He was placed under arrest and transported to the station.

Once at the station, the on-duty detectives told us that one of us had to stay and write a report on our observations and actions. My classmates and I had a hurried conversation. Since I was the only one without a family and children at home, I would stay and do the report. They would pick me up in several hours, and I could try to make up the lost sleep on the ride. They went home to their families, and I sat down with a detective to hammer out a report. Since I didn't even have my own computer access codes, they logged me into a terminal and got me started. The detective outlined what my report should contain, helped me format it, reviewed my completed narrative, and told me that they would add it to the arrest package. I caught a ride home with a patrol officer and tried to snatch some sleep.

A couple of hours later, my classmates picked me up at my apartment, and we started back to training. We were pretty excited. We felt good about having taken action to stop this crime and were proud that we had been able to help our agency. As the ride continued, the excitement quickly passed. We all realized that we might have a slight issue. Despite the fact that the bad guy had been caught and that the detectives had complimented our work, we had a problem. Taking law enforcement action as a Student Officer was a violation of both Academy rules and regulations and state law. We had no idea how this was going to turn out.

We got to our training location and got ready for physical training (PT). As we were warming up and stretching, we discussed the events of the previous evening with our classmates. The class was split in their opinions about what we should have done. Most of the class thought that we should have erred on the side of caution—just watched the guy and called it in. Some of our classmates thought that we had done the right thing. PT was a blur. My head just wasn't in it. At the end of our workout, we traveled back to the academy, got cleaned up and dressed, and headed for the classroom. Just before our morning academic session started, our staff instructor stormed into the classroom. We popped to attention. My heart dropped into my feet as I heard him order the three of us to report to the staff office.

We reported as ordered and stood at attention as the staff informed us that they were aware of our actions from the previous night and were considering what course of action they would take. We had violated the Academy's rules as well as the law governing police training. They ordered us to return to the classroom and await their decision. I remember thinking, as I returned to my desk, that my career was over. We had seen our staff handle discipline with other classmates, and they weren't known for their leniency. If they could kick us out, they would. It was a really long morning. Our classmates were not hopeful about our futures.

Right before lunch, we were summoned back to the staff office. We reported as ordered again and awaited the staff's decision. I'll never forget standing there, looking at the Marine Corps' flag over my staff instructor's shoulder. I felt like a condemned man.

The Academy director started in on us, telling us that he had considered the "facts." He continued, sounding exactly like any self-serving, administrative bureaucrat. He told us that as far as he was concerned, we had broken a major Academy safety rule and that if he had his way, we would be administratively charged and separated from the Academy. I was barely listening as he continued, until I heard that magic word *but.* Any qualification from this uninspiring manager was a potential ray of hope. I started paying close attention again as he went on to tell us that he had just taken a call from one of our captains. When he told us whom he had spoken to, my heart crashed one more time. Allow me to explain.

I had known this captain for over two years and had actually worked for him for the previous two years while employed as a civilian in community policing programs. He was by no means a fan of mine—we really didn't get along. If my career was in his hands, I wasn't overly optimistic. I was probably going to be looking for another job by dinnertime. As I continued to listen, I learned a great deal about the difference between management and leadership. The director, whom I would describe as a classic manager—risk-averse, by the book, and narrowly focused—had made his decision based on minimal facts and written documents. That wasn't surprising. He was a lawyer, appointed to his position following an earlier crisis at the academy. The captain, having adopted a leadership stance, had offered a slightly different opinion. According to the director, our captain had called him to tell him that the department had decided to put the three of us in for commendations. According to the captain, our actions of the previous night were exactly the type of proactive, independent thinking that the department was looking for in new officers. Based on the reports provided to him by the responding patrol officers and detectives, by taking immediate action, we had apprehended the bad guy and recovered the stolen property. When the church members had been informed that the crime was discovered by trainees, they were impressed.

The director concluded his admonition by telling us that despite the fact that he really thought that we should all be kicked out of the Academy, he really couldn't justify taking disciplinary action against three students who were being decorated by their own department. He warned us to watch our steps in the future and stormed out of the office. We stood there, unsure of what our status was, waiting to be dismissed. Only after the door had closed behind the director did our two staff instructors address us. Both staff instructors were working cops. Although they reiterated the director's warning, they did it with a smile and a wink. As they dismissed us to return to our classroom, they congratulated us for having helped our agency clear the case.

I returned to the classroom in a mild state of confusion. How could doing the right thing carry such negative potential consequences? How had my Academy experience and future career been spared by the one individual who, had anyone asked me, I would have been certain would have ruined me? Why did two men in positions of authority have such different and distinct views of the same set of circumstances? Although I didn't recognize it at the time, this episode had clearly drawn the line between management and leadership in my mind. I would think back to the moment in the staff office many times in the coming years when I found myself making difficult decisions.

● ● ● ● ● ● ●

CHAPTER 2

WHAT ABOUT FOLLOWERSHIP?

The word *followership* is not commonly heard in either management or leadership circles. Most people have probably never given followership any thought at all. Yet if you are going to be a leader, you must have followers. If you choose to practice leadership, someone else, of necessity, must practice followership. Whether followership is consciously practiced or occurs by default can make a significant difference in an organization's success or failure. The successes and failures of any organization are often placed at the feet of the organizations' leaders. However, the followers are often as responsible, if not more so, for those results. An organization with inadequate leaders and exceptional followers can still manage to succeed. By the same token, an organization with talented leaders and inept followers will often fail. The followers are critical to the organization's success or failure.

A dictionary definition of the word *followership* is "the capacity or willingness to follow a leader."[8] However, it is not quite as simple as that. Another way to consider effective followership is to regard it as "dynamic subordinancy." That allows us to begin with the understanding that not all followers are static. They do not simply allow themselves to be acted upon by their leaders. Instead, they are dynamic, responding to and changing in regard to the conditions and circumstances around them. How they choose to respond and how we choose to utilize those responses can have a major impact on our ability to lead effectively.

As we start to look at ourselves as leaders, we need to recognize that we have been followers for a long time. We probably spent years as a subordinate before we felt confident enough to make the move into supervision. Additionally, just because we are now serving in a leadership capacity doesn't mean that we aren't still followers. If we are new supervisors, we are still responsible to those officers appointed above us. Even if we rise to the top of our chosen profession and eventually become a chief, commissioner, or superintendent, we will still be responsible to political figures above us. At every level of law enforcement, we are engaged in some type of followership.

The study of followership is a new and fascinating area of academic pursuit. Although it is far too large a topic to be considered fully here, there are two areas of followership with which any new leader must be concerned.

1. What kind of followers do you have working for you? How do you recognize them, and what are the most effective ways of leading them?

2. What kind of follower are you? What kind do you want to be? Your understanding of your own followership style will become critically important when we begin our discussion of leading up.

When developing a short class on leadership for new DEA Basic Agent Trainees (BATs), the Leadership Development Unit stumbled across a clip from the feature film *Gettysburg.* Various other academic institutions and private companies had been using the clip with some success as a leadership lesson. As a matter of fact, in his book *The Leadership Moment,* Michael Useem dedicated a chapter to Colonel Joshua Lawrence Chamberlain's actions during the weeks preceding the battle at Gettysburg as a leadership study. While viewing the clip, I was struck by another behavior that gets little attention in either the movie or the book. It is an outstanding illustration of followership in action.

In the weeks leading up to Gettysburg, Colonel Chamberlain was placed under some immense burdens. His regiment, the 20th Maine, was at less than half strength. On May 24, 1863, he was placed in command of 120 mutineers from the 2nd Maine. These troops would have been a welcome addition to the 20th's troop strength, but they were refusing to fight. Chamberlain's treatment of these men and the speech he made to them shortly after their arrival has become the stuff of legend. It is leadership at its finest.

However, in the movie, another character receives little notice. This character, Captain Clark, is the kind of follower every leader hopes to have. Just as Colonel Chamberlain finishes listening to the grievances from the 2nd Maine's spokesman and right before making the famous speech, he receives word that a courier is arriving in the camp with orders. Chamberlain and his orderly move out to meet the courier. As they do this, another officer approaches, unannounced and without fanfare, and stands directly behind Chamberlain. The colonel receives his orders and returns compliments to his commander. Then he looks over his shoulder and addresses the officer behind him by name. "Captain Clark. You heard him. Get the regiment up. Sound the assembly. Strike the tents."[9] The captain turns to carry out his orders, and Chamberlain promptly moves on to his next task.

The scene receives little notice, but it is remarkable for a couple of reasons. First, Clark appears at Chamberlain's side unbidden. The captain is the kind of officer who recognizes his place in the organization and, as a result, understands that any new orders the regiment receives will require some action on his part. As a result of that understanding, he takes the initiative and places himself in a position where he can best hear the orders and receive additional orders from Colonel Chamberlain. Second, once Chamberlain has issued his orders to Clark, he moves on to another task. He has confidence that Clark will carry out his orders as expected and trusts that the captain will perform his duties in the same fashion that he himself would perform them. Therefore, Chamberlain empowers Captain Clark to get the job done with minimal supervision and no interference. This type of relationship between leader and follower is ideal. Unfortunately, it is only possible with dynamic subordinates who take their role as followers seriously.

Imagine the impact on Colonel Chamberlain's speech to the 2nd Maine if, having received his new orders, he had to turn to his orderly and instruct him to find Captain Clark, then wait for Clark to arrive before passing those orders on. By being an active follower, Captain Clark enabled Colonel Chamberlain to be an effective leader. The two characters complement one another.

TYPES OF FOLLOWERS

In his studies of followers and followership, researcher Robert Kelley categorized followers using two dimensions.[10] The first dimension describes behavior as running from "independent, critical thinking" to "dependent, uncritical thinking." The second dimension describes the followers' level of involvement in their tasks. This scale runs from "active" to "passive." Obviously, the use of these terms makes it easy to envision the ideal follower. An employee who is actively involved in her tasks while being independent and thinking critically is an amazing asset. Conversely, an employee who is passive, dependent, and engaged in uncritical thinking requires constant oversight and supervision. We can easily determine which kind of subordinate we would like to have working with us.

Using his two-dimensional matrix, Kelley placed followers into five distinct categories of behavior. A brief look at each of these followership styles will allow us to evaluate the kind of people we have working for us. Kelley's categories are alienated followers, conformist followers, pragmatist followers, passive followers, and exemplary followers.

Alienated Followers

Alienated followers are characterized as being independent, critical thinkers who are passively involved. They are easily recognizable and are often regarded as cynical. Since they have a streak of independence and do think critically, they may have a lot of knowledge about an organization and its policies, procedures, or management style. However, since they are not actively involved in the organization's mission, they may share this information in negative ways. They may question everything or point out discrepancies between written policy and actions put into practice. Alienated followers are frequently disgruntled. Unfortunately, they may have once been exemplary followers who were burned once too often. They can be incredibly damaging to an organization and its goals.

Any organization will have alienated followers. In a law enforcement agency, they are easy to recognize. These are the mission-driven officers who may have really believed they could change the world. Early in their careers, they sought challenging assignments or membership in special squads or units. They may have suggested changes or improvements for the good of the organization. Eventually, after continued rejection or failure, their enthusiasm waned. They grew wary of their superiors failing to support them and their peers accusing them of "kissing up." Operationally, they may practice "FIDO" policing. The concept of "F— It, Drive On" policing is a manner of withholding discretionary effort. Alienated officers may come to believe that going the extra mile or intervening in an observed incident will only subject them to further rejection or ridicule. If they aren't dispatched to it, they aren't going to handle it. Since they had been highly motivated, they probably learned a lot about the policy manual, the rules and regulations, and the contract. Armed with this knowledge and incredibly frustrated, they can become an immensely negative influence on the workforce. Alienated followers can be brought back into the organizational fold if they can be successfully engaged. Their active involvement in organizational goals may return some of their productivity.

Conformist Followers

Conformist followers are identified as being actively involved in the organization but as being dependent, uncritical thinkers. They are universally known as "yes men." These are the followers who will accept or buy into any new program or model and follow orders willingly—without thought or consideration. Conformist followers can be valuable during uncommon, critical incidents. However, during normal operations, the lack of critical thinking leads to a type of groupthink. They will follow the company line because it is the company line, even if the obvious result is failure. Some organizations create conformist followers by hammering employees into a rigid command structure under authoritarian supervisors.

Conformist followers are also easy to recognize. They are the officers who will accept any order, instruction, policy, or new program "because the chief said so." They will not stop to question the benefits or costs of the change. Even if they do question it to themselves, they will support it outwardly. Conformist followers have the attitude "If they want apples, give them apples."

Pragmatist Followers

Pragmatist followers fall in the middle of the continuum along both dimensions. These are the employees who do not want to stand out; they tend to "fly below the radar." Their performance is minimally adequate, and they avoid both trouble and excellence. Their goal is simply to survive their career. Pragmatists will avoid taking a stand on issues and may play both sides of the coin to avoid commitment. Since they occupy the middle of the follower matrix, they impede movement in any direction.

Pragmatist followers are recognized as stumbling blocks in organizations. In a law enforcement agency, they may be the staff officers who are so concerned with the policy manual that they are incapable of practical action. They may delay a decision on a matter until they get the concurrence of all the affected parties, even if the matter is time-sensitive and the delay will cost a significant opportunity. Pragmatists are risk-averse and do not like to take chances. Operationally, these are the officers who will work their entire shift and answer their calls but avoid initiating citizen contacts. They may practice what has become known as "NCNC" policing. The acronym, which stands for "No Contact, No Complaint," illustrates the pragmatist point of view: if I don't do anything, I can't get into trouble.

Passive Followers

Passive followers are characterized by passive involvement and dependent, uncritical thinking. These followers must be told what to do and when to do it. As a result, they require constant supervision and direction. They display no initiative and are incapable of self-starting. Unfortunately, some passive followers are created by organizations with authoritarian bosses. They behave the way they are expected to behave by their superiors.

Passive followers are easy to recognize. These are the employees who wait to be acted upon. When handling a call, they will wait for a supervisor or a more experienced (or more confident) officer to make a decision. Instead of being decisive and taking action, they wait for someone to direct them and force them to action. Passive followers are not unknown in law enforcement. Unfortunately, there really isn't any place for them in the field. Law enforcement requires decisiveness. If you cannot make a decision, you can't do the job.

Exemplary Followers

Exemplary followers are characterized by active involvement in the organization's tasks and a high degree of independence and critical thought. These employees are the self-starters who take the initiative and make things happen around them. Exemplary followers are involved in and committed to the mission of the organization. On the other hand, they are willing to ask the hard questions. They will stand up to their superiors—not to be obstructionist but to ensure that the best actions are being implemented. Exemplary followers are interested in promoting the entire organization.

Police agencies often have difficulty accommodating exemplary followers. The officers who request the additional training, offer risky suggestions, or recommend new tactics and equipment are often viewed as advancing their own agendas. The typical, management-driven response to these officers is often, "We've never had a problem doing it the old way. Why should we change now?" Unfortunately, that type of response runs the risk of turning the exemplary follower into the alienated follower, and we've already seen the negative results of that transition.

Having categorized the above classes of followers, it would appear obvious what kind of followers we, as supervisors, would hope for. Self-starters, who take the initiative, make everyone's job easier. The more difficult questions are these: What kind of follower are you? If you are not an exemplary follower, would you like to become one? If so, how do you begin?

Once we recognize that followership is a valid half of the leader/ subordinate equation, we need to ask ourselves what the follower's job is. The short, simple answer is that the follower's job is to do what the boss requests or demands. This simplistic approach is troubling, however. What if the boss's requests or demands are clearly wrong? What if they are illegal or immoral? What is the follower's job then? The question isn't simple. Neither is the answer. In the extreme view, the follower's job is to perform those actions or tasks that further the organization's overall mission. That job carries with it a lot of diverse responsibilities, each of them important.

At the very basic level, a follower is responsible for himself. In this day and age of blame placing, that is not a popular sentiment. However, it cannot be dismissed. As an individual, I am responsible for myself. I am responsible for my own attitude, behaviors, actions, performance, and success. I cannot control all of the circumstances or conditions that surround me, but I can control how I respond to them. The minute I abdicate my individual responsibility to someone else, I have ceased to be an effective follower.

The next thing that a follower is responsible for is her own understanding of the job. If I don't know what my job is, I can't be expected to perform it well. Unfortunately, many passive followers or conformist followers will receive a task or job description, quickly and quietly acknowledge it, and appear to understand the assignment. Without seeking clarification, they begin the task while misunderstanding it. This continues until something goes wrong. Then both the follower and the supervisor are frustrated. The follower feels that the task wasn't explained well enough. The boss feels that the follower should have sought clarification or asked questions. Many times, the fault for the misunderstanding is placed with the supervisor. However, the follower is the one who knew she did not fully grasp the task. It is the responsibility of the follower, in the role of the producer, to obtain specific information. Questions like "What is my task?" "What are your expectations of my performance?" "What will my rewards or compensation be if I perform at that level?" and "What will the consequences be if I don't?" need to be clarified by the follower. Effective, exemplary followers ask these questions to avoid confusion.

A follower is also responsible for his knowledge of the job. A passive follower will assume that if the organization wants better performance, then the organization will offer better training or incentives. Dynamic, exemplary followers look at this from a different point of view. They understand that their skill and professionalism has value. They also understand that it belongs to them. Exemplary followers actively seek to improve their skills and enhance their job performance. They request additional training and welcome new work assignments that will expand their expertise. Exemplary followers treat their chosen trade as a profession. For law enforcement professionals, this attitude may show up in several ways. They may request and attend advanced training or join professional organizations and associations. Many exemplary followers seek a better understanding of the industry of law enforcement by reading law enforcement-specific books and periodicals. They seek to increase the value and marketability of their skills and experience.

Understanding the job and having the skills to perform the job allow effective followers to do the job well. This is the next responsibility of followers—to fulfill their functions and complete the mission. However, mission accomplishment performed in a vacuum does not accomplish all that we need done. While the follower is responsible for the outcome of the task, the leader is still responsible for the coordination of that outcome with other processes within the agency. For that reason, effective followers keep their supervisors informed by being accessible and using effective communications. In this way, supervisors are aware that the job tasks are understood and are being approached with the right skills and tools and that progress is being made. By keeping their superiors informed, effective followers allow their bosses to see one more part of the big picture. They encourage their bosses to be empowering and supportive simultaneously. They also allow their supervisors to bring additional resources to bear quickly.

Followership is a relatively new, even foreign, concept. Yet in any great organization, effective leaders are supported by effective followers. As new supervisors, it is essential that we recognize the followership styles of our troops. Those who can be corrected through training or coaching should be. Eventually, we want all of our followers to be exemplary followers.

Having learned to recognize the followership styles of our subordinates, we next need to turn our attention to ourselves. What kind of follower have we been? What kind will we be in the future? Are we supporting our organization's goals and missions? If not, what do we have to do to become an exemplary follower?

There are no leaders without followers. Leaders without effective followers are handicapped. On the other hand, when both sides of the equation are putting forth a full effort, the entire organization is better off.

I offer another "war story" to illustrate some of the problems that can occur when follower styles clash, particularly between followers of different ranks.

• • • • • • •

As a young patrol officer, I had the good fortune to serve as an assistant team leader on our Special Response Team (SRT). This placed me in the unusual position of being junior in both rank and experience but having supervisory responsibility in some instances when the team deployed.

Independence Day turned out to be a beautiful summer day in the Berkshires. As a police officer, however, my holiday was less than perfect. I had worked the midnight shift, then immediately taken a traffic post for the Fourth of July parade. After the parade, anticipating another overnight shift, I decided to go home and get some sleep. After a couple of hours, I was awakened by my phone. I answered and quickly learned how I was going to be spending the rest of my holiday.

An irate citizen had become distressed by the loud music and fireworks in his neighborhood. In response, he had exited his apartment with a shotgun, brandished it at his neighbors, threatened them, and retreated back into his apartment. Patrol had responded, contained the scene, and attempted to contact the suspect. No contact had been established, and the Special Response Team was being activated. As my adrenaline surged, I kitted up, rolled out, and headed for the scene. On the way, I received a couple of phone calls. One of my team leaders was out of town at a concert and wasn't sure how soon he could make it back. The second had a family situation and was going to respond but might be delayed. As a result, I was tasked with coordinating the initial tactical response to the location and liaising with the patrol units on scene.

As I turned into the neighborhood, I was encouraged to see that the street had been closed down. I proceeded to one end of the street and started looking for the command post. As I was doing this, I observed the on-duty street supervisor. He was pacing back and forth in front of what I would soon discover was the target house. I was more than a little concerned. He was pacing in the line of fire and did not appear to be in contact with the command post.

As near as I could tell, the initial responding officers had identified the problem. Most of them had then pulled back to establish a perimeter and lock down the street. Command officers had arrived and set up a command post at the end of the street. Newly arriving assets were reporting there and receiving briefing information. However, some patrol units were still in proximity to the target. Their sergeant had arrived on scene but was not coordinating their deployment. Instead, he was pacing in front of the target, exposing himself to potential fire and not providing information on his officers' locations to the command staff. As a result, replacing patrol officers with tactical officers on the inner perimeter would not be easy.

I informed the sergeant of the potential problem. It should have been a simple interaction. He would take note of the positions of his deployed officers, then proceed to the command post and inform the planning officers of the positions. After that, he would remain in the command post to advocate for his men and to make sure that they were properly relieved from their posts. Instead, he acknowledged my concern, then turned and walked in the opposite direction and away from the command post. I'm not sure if I saw him again that evening. Instead, I returned to the command post, and once our team leaders arrived on scene, we started initiating a relief in place. The patrol officers were eventually replaced with tactical officers, and the operation proceeded. I never discovered where the sergeant had gone.

Much later, I would analyze this sergeant's actions as part of my leadership studies. Eventually, I concluded that this particular sergeant was a good example of a passive follower. In the absence of clear directives from a superior officer, he had been unwilling to decide on any course of action. His indecisiveness manifested itself in his pacing. Even the decision to seek cover or concealment wasn't being made. This sergeant was not receiving direction from his superior officers, because they were working on a different set of problems and were expecting him to take action to resolve the containment issue. When Special Response Team assets arrived on the scene, he turned the containment issue over to us and moved on to another project without providing us with essential information.

• • • • • • •

CHAPTER 3

COMMON QUALITIES
OF A LEADER

"Do the right thing, because it's the right thing to do."

There is no way that I can provide one, simple, catch-all definition of what makes a "good" leader. Leadership is indeed an art, and the styles of practicing it are as varied as styles of painting, music, sculpture, or any other art. And although leadership defies categorization and definition, we intrinsically realize when someone is a good leader and when someone is not. We also recognize that not all good leaders are good all of the time. Conversely, we know that bad leaders have their occasional moments of greatness. Instead of lending itself to a simple definition, effectiveness as a leader seems to be made up of the right combination of a wide variety of characteristics and behaviors. When these factors combine in the right proportions and the good qualities outweigh the bad, we describe the practitioner as a good leader. I had the good fortune to experience a good leader in the U.S. Navy.

• • • • • • •

In 1988, when I reported to the U.S. Naval Academy, one member of my training cadre was a highly motivated Midshipman Second Class. Obviously to his face, we addressed him by his rank and name, but behind his back, this young officer was always referred to as "Johnny O." Johnny O had just returned to Annapolis from Quantico, Virginia, where he had gone through "Bulldog." Bulldog was the six-week introduction to the Marine Corps that was conducted for Academy and ROTC midshipmen contemplating a Marine Corps career. He was very passionate about his responsibilities for training us. He also never passed on an opportunity to educate us about the world according to Johnny O.

I distinctly remember one evening out on the drill field. The sun was setting over the Severn, and Johnny O placed us in a "school circle" with his customary order of "Sit, kneel, bend!" In this way, all four squads could see and hear him while he waxed eloquent on the day's lesson. He began by explaining to us that in our careers, we would be afforded the opportunity to observe a wide variety of leaders and supervisors. Some we would like, and some we would dislike. However, each would have specific qualities that we would find admirable, useful, or valuable. Each would also have qualities we found disreputable and counterproductive. He challenged us to imagine ourselves holding two giant laundry bags. One was to hold all of the good qualities of the leaders we observed. The other was for all of the bad qualities. As we made observations, he told us, our task was to fill the good bag with all of the qualities we wanted to emulate and the bad bag with all of the qualities we wanted to avoid. Periodically, we were to discard the contents of the bad bag. However, as we built our own style of leadership, we were to reach into the good bag for the building blocks.

Johnny O's "good bag/bad bag" leadership lesson struck a particular chord with me, and I've held it dear. Over the past several years, I've attempted to put quite a few qualities into my own good bag. Some of them have been added more than once, as I've observed the same trait in a wide range of leaders. I've chosen some of the more frequent and important ones as the basis of this chapter.

• • • • • • •

COMPETENT

Effective leaders are competent. They not only have the basic skills to do their own job, they possess advanced skills and the skills to perform other jobs. They may not necessarily be experts in every aspect of their organization, but they are knowledgeable about a variety of aspects. They are able to discuss all of their organization's involvements intelligently and with understanding. A good leader must be able to convey to his troops the sentiment that he will never ask them to do anything that he has not already done or would not be willing to do. This is an essential element of leadership by example, which will be discussed in greater detail later.

Not only does a good leader possess competence, she allows herself to be seen improving that competence. The good leader cultivates a reputation as someone who is constantly seeking to expand her skills and knowledge. The effective leader does not seek to become just a skilled practitioner but to advance to be a qualified instructor. There is no better way to demonstrate competencies than to teach those skills to another.

Achieving this level of competency in basic skills can be very important for a leader. Even management textbooks say that one of a supervisor's primary responsibilities is to train his people. This training can occur in a formal setting or in informal interaction on the job. A supervisor who is not constantly providing some level of training to his troops is dooming them to repeat the same mistakes. In a law enforcement agency, this can be an invitation to liability. As important as the role of trainer is for a manager, it is doubly important for a leader. By training and teaching his people, a leader demonstrates concern for their well-being, their development, and their future.

CONFIDENT

Effective leaders exude confidence. Confidence is an often maligned character trait that can be mistaken for arrogance or excessive ego. Although these traits may appear similar and even related, confidence is not necessarily accompanied by ego or arrogance. Instead, confidence is the knowledge, or faith, that one has the ability, the skills, the desire, and the mind-set to succeed. Confidence is knowing that you can accomplish those tasks set before you or obtain the means to accomplish them.

Confidence is made possible partially by knowing and recognizing your limitations. A confident person knows when a task is beyond her abilities because confidence allows her to say so. Therefore, the confident person doesn't necessarily believe that she can do anything, but she does know exactly what she can do.

The confident leader imparts his confidence to his subordinates. Followers are more inclined to place their faith in the confident leader, because that leader always seems to know what he is doing. The quality of confidence is partly based in the quality of competence. Being a competent practitioner of your trade allows you to have confidence in your abilities. These two traits, competence and confidence, are frequently mentioned in roundtable discussions of the qualities that are desirable in a leader.

CARING

The personal characteristic of caring, or compassion, is perhaps one of the most misunderstood aspects of leadership. Inexperienced supervisors allow themselves to be persuaded that if they show compassion, then they are weak. They allow themselves to believe that to be a strong leader, they must be authoritative, forceful, and standoffish. Then they wonder why their people don't perform at high levels for them.

Caring is not a weakness. It is instead a fundamental strength. All of the aspects of leadership discussed above also relate to caring. As stated in the introduction, leadership is about your people. At its roots, it is about caring for them. Effective leaders demonstrate concern and compassion for their subordinates, their colleagues, and their bosses. In doing so, they do not appear weak. They do it to inspire loyalty, trust, and mutual respect.

One particular element of caring is fairness. One survey of over 55,000 law enforcement officers found that the top three characteristics they desired in their leaders were "honest," "fair," and "cares about me." Caring encompasses all of these to some extent, but fairness is a little different. Many leaders assume that treating people fairly means treating them all the same. According to Ken Blanchard, however, true fairness means treating each person as they deserve to be treated. The equal treatment of unequal performers is inherently unfair. If we truly care about our troops, we must treat them fairly. That requires us to recognize how they deserve to be treated and to be consistent in our treatment of similar behaviors.

Effective leaders care about their troops' current needs. Are they adequately compensated? Are they told they are appreciated? Are they properly trained? Do they have the equipment they need? They also care about their situations outside of work. Is my officer distracted by something in his personal life? Are my people maintaining healthy lifestyles? Are they taking care of their other responsibilities? They also care about their people's futures. Am I providing my troops with the necessary skills to advance? Am I training and teaching them to succeed? Am I providing for my agency's continued success by developing tomorrow's leaders?

Dr. Kevin Gilmartin teaches the concept of "emotional survival." As a leader, if I care about my troops, I must recognize what effect their career has had on them. In his book *Emotional Survival for Law Enforcement,* Gilmartin describes an effect that he terms the "emotional rollercoaster." This psychological effect results from officers working in a high-stress environment. As a result of their immersion in the law enforcement lifestyle and culture, officers normally undergo significant personal and psychological changes. According to Gilmartin, the first major change normally takes about five years to set in. As a leader, am I aware of what is happening to my troops? Do I care enough about them to discuss these changes and to help them deal with them? Am I looking out for their emotional survival with the same passion that I look out for their physical survival?

All of these questions are expressions of caring. When you look at it this way, you can see that caring is a strength rather than a weakness. In the book *Managing From the Heart,* authors Hyler Bracey, Jack Rosenblum, Aubrey Sanford, and Roy Trueblood develop a five-step approach to looking at caring as a strength. During one discussion regarding the effects of caring on productivity, their character Selena states,

> It's very simple. People are more productive and perform at their best when they feel good about themselves and when they feel good about

what they do. It's impossible for individuals to feel really good about themselves and what they're doing if they are constantly being told they are wrong. To be productive, people need to be told what they're doing that's right and how their work is making a worthwhile contribution to something. People like to be told they are a contributing part of a winning team.[11]

Another aspect of caring has to do with really knowing your subordinates as people. One part of caring is communication. (We will discuss communication again as a skill in its own right later in this chapter.) In a presentation to a group of narcotics supervisors, Dr. Harvey Goldstein of the Halen Group described what he referred to as the "Platinum Rule." This concept, first advanced by Dr. Tony Allesandra of PeopleSmart, suggests a more effective way of communicating with people. Going a step farther than the Golden Rule, treating others as you wish to be treated, the Platinum Rule suggests treating others as *they* wish to be treated. How do you accomplish that? You care enough to find out something about them and their concerns. You care about them as individuals.

Displaying caring as a leader will do much to enhance your ability to get the job done. As stated in *Managing From the Heart,* "When people feel you care about them and won't crush them, they are much more willing to listen to you and learn from you, because they want to avoid mistakes and accomplish more."[12] That kind of attitude greatly advances mission accomplishment.

Sometimes, the notion of caring for our people gets lost in the clutter of operational demands. It is all too easy to get caught up in the middle of running an operation and stop thinking about the needs and well-being of our officers. The following two stories illustrate how easily it can happen.

• • • • • • •

Several years ago, I was assigned as the desk sergeant on a cold winter day. In our organization, we normally attempt to assign two sergeants to each shift. The first, the desk sergeant, is assigned to the front desk and is responsible for station security, communications, prisoners, and administrative functions. The second, if working, is assigned as the street supervisor and is responsible for coordinating the efforts of our field units. Under normal circumstances, the desk sergeant doesn't leave the station. On the other hand, in the case of an extreme emergency, the desk sergeant can deploy into the field.

On this particular day, I was not only assigned to the desk, but I was also junior to the street supervisor by several years. The day was rapidly coming to a close, and it was beginning to get dark. As is often the case in law enforcement, our nice quiet day was suddenly shattered. Our communications center received a holdup alarm from a small, local bank. This particular bank had only one branch, a stand-alone building, in the middle of a large, commercial parking lot on the far outskirts of town. The alarm was confirmed. The bank had been robbed at gunpoint, and multiple patrol units were dispatched as the initial response.

As the response was en route, I took up a position in the communications center to coordinate our units and arrange for additional resources. Investigative units from the Detective Bureau and Crime Scene Services responded from the station with their commanding officer. Our chief notified us that he was responding. As all of this occurred, I looked behind me to see my partner, the street supervisor, standing in the communications center. Essentially, numerous police assets were converging on a critical incident, and the person with the primary responsibility for coordinating the initial on-scene response was standing several miles away, with me. I was dumbfounded.

The incident progressed quickly, with investigative units assuming control of the scene at the bank. Interviews were conducted, and information on the suspects was developed. The chief and the detective captain established command and control at the bank. Patrol units rapidly returned to their cruisers and started scouring the immediate area for armed suspects and a getaway vehicle. Then things got really interesting.

Within a very short time, uniforms developed a detailed vehicle description and expanded the area search. In one of those all-too-common combinations of highly motivated police officers and pure luck, a young rookie officer found the suspect vehicle behind an apartment building less than a mile away. She radioed in her discovery and requested additional units. The patrol officers converged on the second scene and contained a new perimeter. To my amazement, as this second scene was still developing, my partner, the street supervisor, changed out of his uniform and went home at shift change.

As all of this was going on, we received a call from one of the officers on scene. He was not the senior officer, but he was the most qualified to supervise, based on training and experience. He informed me that he had a half dozen officers holding containment on the car and an adjacent apartment building. They were deployed between the buildings and in the tree line. Additionally, the media had learned about the second scene and were now moving from the bank to the apartment complex. They were demanding an update and were attempting to break containment to get photos and video. The officer on scene couldn't coordinate the containment and deal with the media. He reasonably expected some help.

My agency does not have formal "delegation of authority." Technically, our line officers are prohibited from assuming supervisory positions, according to their collective bargaining contract. Despite the contract, I told the officer on the phone that he was the scene commander until relieved. I immediately contacted the units at the bank and attempted to speak with the chief. Of course, I didn't get the chief. Instead, the detective captain returned my call and told me that he would take care of whatever I needed. Unfortunately, I didn't need protocols from the detective captain. What I needed was someone, preferably the agency head, to take the media pressure off of my patrol units so they could focus on the mission. I tactfully let the captain know that I had asked for the chief and I needed the chief. Fortunately, I got the chief on the phone, and to his credit, he immediately left the bank and headed for the apartment complex.

By this time, shift change had finished, and the evening shift staff was coming on. Evenings had no sergeant assigned to the street supervisor position. As soon as my relief came on duty, I told him that unless he had an objection, I was heading out to the apartment complex to check on my people. I changed my clothes into cold weather gear and headed to the scene. When I got there, both the chief and the captain had finished with the media and proceeded down to the inner perimeter. Since the units on perimeter had responded with their cruisers, most of the evening shift units were still stranded at the station without transportation. This was a problem, since the robbery had tapped most of our resources and service calls were stacking up. As a result, the brass had formed a plan. Evening units would carpool out to our scene, collect their cars and start answering calls. That was fine, as far as it went, but the plan was to leave my people on their perimeter positions.

This is when I started to lose my patience. First, we had a supervisor allow his people to respond to a critical incident while he concentrated on making it home on time. Next, we put line officers in the position of having to compromise their operational security, because collectively, we couldn't provide them with a supervisor to handle the media crush. Now, I was dealing with a redeployment plan that ignored some pretty important factors. Remember, it was the middle of winter in New England. The temperature had been below freezing all day and had been dropping steadily since the sun went down. My people had been on scene for nearly an hour by this time, and most of them were outside in the subfreezing temperatures. Some of them had responded without adequate cold weather gear, and they were starting to get hypother-mic. While my officers had been suffering in the cold, the armed sus-pects had been resting inside a heated apartment. Despite all of this, my supervisors were not planning to relieve our field assets.

I asked to speak with the chief and requested permission to initi-ate a call-out of the Special Response Team. I pointed out to him that when team assets arrived, they would show up with appropriate cold weather gear, water, food, and weaponry for a protracted perimeter operation. Once I pointed this out to the chief, he was all for it. It wasn't that anyone consciously wanted the day shift officers to suffer. Everyone had been busy running the investigation, and the officers' welfare simply hadn't been a consideration.

• • • • • • •

During a subsequent operation, I was the one who got caught up in operational planning and failed to account for all of my officers' needs. Early in the morning on Christmas Eve, I was sleep-ing soundly when my pager started chirping on the bedside table. I checked the screen and realized that this holiday wasn't going to go as planned, either. I called the station to get more information and was informed that it was an out-of-town call-out for a barricaded subject. We were being deployed to a small town at the far northern edge of the county. The local police department had received information that a distraught individual had threatened to do harm to himself. They had requested assistance from one of their neighboring departments. Among the officers responding to the mutual aid request were two members of our countywide Special Response Team. The officers had assembled and started to approach the house. As they were approach-ing, they heard gunshots from inside the house. They had pulled back and contained the target house. The two SRT members had suggested to the local police chief that he request the Special Response Team. The request had been approved, and we were going.

I got dressed and left for the station. The target location was over 20 miles away, and we were going to travel as a unit. As I drove, freezing rain was falling and covering the roads with a layer of black ice. At the station, team members collected and loaded equipment into the necessary vehicles. Within a short time, we were loaded out and traveling north as fast as the road conditions would allow.

We arrived on scene and were met by the police chief. He briefed us on the situation and told us that there was a state police Special Tactics and Operations (STOP) team en route also. We started deploying resources for a perimeter containment operation. The freezing rain was still falling, and there was a deep blanket of snow on the ground. Soon after we arrived, the STOP team arrived on scene also. We coordinated our efforts, split up certain responsibilities, and developed a schedule to exchange assets on the perimeter.

During our initial deployment onto the perimeter, we had relieved most of the initial responding patrol officers. However, our two team members were left on the perimeter as part of our containment team. All of our newly deployed officers were dressed out in insulated long underwear, tactical uniforms, waterproof outerwear, and, if necessary, snow overwhites. We scheduled the first perimeter exchange for 45 minutes.

A few minutes after the perimeter had been established, I received a radio call from one of the out-of-town team members who had initiated the callout. I could practically hear his teeth chattering as he inquired if there was a plan for his partner and him to be relieved. The realization of my idiocy struck me like a slap in the face. The officers that we had deployed were dressed and equipped for a prolonged, cold-weather perimeter operation, and 45 minutes would be no problem for them. However, the first two team members on scene had responded in patrol gear. They had been in their positions since before my pager had awoken me in my warm bed. That was over an hour ago. Those guys were freezing.

We quickly made arrangements to replace them on the perimeter. They came back in, briefed us on their role in the operation up to that point, and warmed up. As soon as they got warm, they changed into their tactical gear and joined the rest of the team as we continued with the operation.

Once again, it became painfully apparent how easy it was to overlook the needs and well-being of your people when operational demands started mounting up. Once we had assumed responsibility for the perimeter, those officers became my responsibility. However, because I already regarded them as my operators, I grouped them in with the rest of the perimeter assets in our scheduling plan. It had never occurred to me to account for their prior involvement in the operation. Fortunately for me, they were both the type of exemplary followers who had no issues with reminding me of my responsibilities.

• • • • • • •

ETHICAL

Perhaps no single topic or phrase elicits a more negative response from law enforcement students than the topic of ethics. Yet ethics is inescapably part of our law enforcement mission. When discussing leadership, we do not want to get caught up in the detailed minutiae of ethics that is so common in entry-level law enforcement training. Instead, we want to look at the big picture.

One would hope that anyone selected as a leader in a law enforcement agency, or any other organization for that matter, would be an ethical person. We want our leaders to have personal honor and integrity. On some level, we may just assume that they do. Colonel McKnight relates an episode during his leadership presentation regarding just this matter. During a presentation to an ROTC group, the colonel was addressing the seven values of the U.S. Army. A ROTC cadet asked the colonel which of the seven was the most important. Colonel McKnight says that after some consideration, he discarded honor and integrity and responded with "respect." He explains that all seven are very important. However, he assumes that all leaders in the army are going to have honor and integrity, but they might still need to work on mutual respect. Honor and integrity are such fundamental aspects of any successful leader's persona, that we may just discount them.

What about our newly promoted supervisor? Yesterday, as a patrol officer, her idea of integrity revolved around some relatively simple concepts: Don't take free coffee. Don't accept discount meals. Don't nap on the midnight shift. Don't agree to fix tickets. Don't make exceptions to the law. Her ethical training in the police academy was situational. It all followed this pattern: in this situation, do or don't do this. Now as a supervisor, the officer's ethical concerns will be larger and involve much more serious consequences. Is the officer prepared? We believe so. If we didn't, we probably wouldn't have promoted her.

Fortunately, ethics is something that is better understood with a simple explanation rather than a complicated one. At the Naval Academy, one of my upperclassmen narrowed it down to this: "Do the right thing, because it's the right thing to do." One sentence. Eleven words. It is a fairly complete explanation of ethics and integrity. We all came to law enforcement with some ethical training. It came from our parents, our families, our teachers, our religious leaders, and our communities. We recognize the difference between right and wrong, and most of the time can determine which action will be the right one. Essentially, ethical behavior is the behavior that makes the right decision.

If our subordinates have faith that we will always do our best to make the right decision, they will feel more comfortable in attaching their lot to ours. If they know we can be trusted to do the right thing and not place them and the agency in jeopardy, then they will feel justified in following us and supporting us, no matter the cost. If they believe we will always make decisions with their greater good in mind, they will empower us to act on their behalf. If not, they will act in their own best interests, maybe to the detriment to the mission and the organization.

By treating ethics simply, we avoid the need to belabor the details of particular situations. However, one situation does deserve particular mention. In most law enforcement ethics classes, this issue would receive no consideration, yet as a leader, it is profoundly valuable. While discussing integrity, Stephen Covey addresses a specific type of loyalty. Covey says,

> One of the most important ways to manifest integrity is to *be loyal to those who are not present.* In doing so, we build the trust of those who are present. When you defend those who are absent, you retain the trust of those present.[13]

Essentially, Covey is discussing talking about people behind their back. No matter whom you are talking to, if you bad-mouth someone else to her, she will find herself wondering what you are saying about her when she is absent. A better approach is to defend people when they are absent, building the trust of those to whom you are talking. This small investment can do a lot to enhance your reputation for personal integrity.

This simplistic approach to integrity may seem elementary. However, it is enough to allow the effective practice of leadership. Do the right thing. Not for the advancement, the glory, or the money. Do it because it is the right thing to do. Gain a reputation for acting "rightly." Protect that reputation. Allow others to feel comfortable in the knowledge that you can be trusted to act this way all of the time.

One of the most difficult situations that I've ever faced as a police supervisor had nothing to do with operations. Instead, it was a matter of administrative policy and personal ethics. The ramifications and long-lasting aftereffects are still being felt within our organization.

• • • • • • •

While I was on my assignment with the DEA, any time I came home, I tried to spend some time with the officers with whom I'd worked on my shift, on the SRT, or in the training unit. We would usually try to have dinner or a cookout during each of my home visits. During one of these visits, I became aware that one of the female officers on my shift was having some difficulties with another supervisor. No one wanted to tell me what the problem was, and anytime I asked, I was told that it was being taken care of.

At the end of the year, I came home and resumed my duties as a shift supervisor. Shortly after returning to work, I noticed that this woman was having a really tough time. She was taking an unusual amount of sick time and appeared to be very unhappy. Any attempt I made to provide assistance was met with resistance and assurances that she could take care of it. At one point, she actually asked me to promise that I wouldn't intervene without her permission.

Not long after that conversation, another officer approached me and told me that the supervisor had touched the female officer in an inappropriate manner. Although I knew what the law required of me as a supervisor, I was still conflicted. On the one hand, the officer had asked me not to take action on her behalf. On the other hand, the supervisor was someone with whom I had worked closely over a number of years. We had worked and trained together in a number of capacities.

The following morning, I reported to work early and met with the senior lieutenant. This supervisor was someone I regarded as the most ethical person in the department, and I knew she wouldn't steer me wrong. The lieutenant listened patiently as I outlined the entire chain of events and told me that I knew what I had to do. I'd known all along, but I needed to hear it from someone else. I immediately wrote a detailed report of the information I had received and hand-delivered it to the chief. Within a matter of minutes, the officer was summoned to the chief's office. What followed was the beginning of one of the most difficult episodes in my law enforcement career. Before it was over, the department would be divided, new policies would be created, some officers would leave the agency, and others would be fired.

Throughout it all, I would be plagued by a series of doubts. Should I have known earlier? Could I have done more? Was I right to break my word to my officer? What about my colleague—did I owe him something more? At the end of the day, I know only one thing: I did what was right for me, because it was the right thing to do.

● ● ● ● ● ●

COMMUNICATIVE

Effective and skilled leaders understand the value of communication in all of its forms. Exemplary leaders work to become gifted communicators. Many types of communication can be critically important in the practice of leadership: conversations, speeches, training sessions, written reports, press releases, and many others. Every one of these may be important to a leader. However, for the newly promoted supervisor, supervising a small unit, the stock in trade of good leadership is oral communication.

Oral communication is the most common style of communication practiced by small-unit leaders. Although oral communication seems straightforward, it is actually composed of several distinct components. Each part is important, but they are not equally important. If any part of oral communication can be said to be most important to leaders, it is *listening*.

The best leaders are skilled, empathic listeners. Note: Not just listeners, but empathic listeners. This means that they not only hear what is being said to them, they acknowledge it and return it to the speaker in such a way as to let the speaker know he has been understood. Covey describes this practice this way: "Seek first to understand, then to be understood."[14] He refers to this, his Fifth Habit, as "empathic listening." In *Managing From the Heart,* the authors describe the practice as "Hear and understand me."[15] They refer to it as a "listening check."

This behavior goes beyond "actively listening." It is not enough to hear the speaker's words. Empathic listening requires the listener to hear the words, ask pointed questions, and read the speaker's expressions and posture, all to divine the true message being delivered. It requires the listener to respond to the speaker so that the speaker recognizes that the message has been received and fully understood. It requires time and energy to practice empathic listening. However, the payoff can be enormous.

According to Dr. Harvey Goldstein, empathy is an amazing tool. Dr. Goldstein, a clinical psychologist, instructs blocks on crisis management for the DEA. During his discussions, he points out that positron emissions testing (PET) scans have revealed that empathy causes the release of serotonin in the brain. Serotonin is a chemical transmitter that causes people to feel good and calms them down. According to Dr. Goldstein, by being empathic to somebody who is speaking to us, we can alter his brain chemistry and his behavior. This may explain why people always feel better after "face time" with a good boss. Our empathic listening can make our troops feel better at the time and feel better about coming to us in the future.

The other elements of oral communication are also important. Good listeners recognize that only a small percentage of a message is communicated by words. The rest is conveyed by postures, gestures, tone, inflection, proximity, and other "intangibles." Skilled listeners are adept at picking up on all of these in search of complete meaning. Collectively, these elements are often lumped together under the collective term of "body language." The ability to read body language is critical to successful oral communication.

Finally, oral communication is also about the words. Leaders should strive to increase and improve their vocabulary. They should avoid off-color language in their professional contacts. Work-related jargon is fine when dealing with colleagues but should be avoided when speaking with the general public or the press. Leaders attempt to convey their messages in powerful and positive terms. Choosing the right words can help them do this.

One particular type of oral communication demands special attention. Perhaps the most poorly utilized and wasted form of communication is the meeting. According to Charles Thompson, executives attend over 11 million meetings a day in the United States, and over 70 million meetings are held every day worldwide.[16] Many of these meetings bog down in details and minutiae. This doesn't have to be the case, however. In his book *Leadership,* Rudy Giuliani, the former mayor of New York City, describes his philosophy on meetings. According to Mayor Giuliani, he started nearly every day of his administration with an eight o'clock "morning meeting." All of his core staff and department heads were required to attend. The meetings lasted between 45 and 90 minutes. Each person at the table was required to share any pertinent information regarding his department or agency. Giuliani further describes his meetings this way:

> The morning meeting was the core of my approach to managing. It served numerous purposes—decision-making, communicating, even socializing—but most of all, it kept me accountable. The morning meeting was where the chief executive was responsible and could hold everybody else responsible. Those present could go back to their agencies and act in a similar way. Instead of trying to protect themselves against the risk of a bad decision, they were willing to make decisions, knowing that a few might end up being wrong, but at least things got done, and in reasonable time.[17]

Regarding the actual utility of his morning meetings, Mayor Giuliani describes their tangible results:

> My mayoral staff knew that they would see me at a specific time and place every day. Executives of all types, even the mayor of New York City, have been known to hide behind a phalanx of secretaries and assistants, leaving underlings twisting in the wind. A daily meeting, in which everyone is entitled to air concerns, meant my staff knew they could get a yes or no from the boss. They knew they could tell whoever was waiting for that yes or no that they would definitely see me the next day. And even if the issue could not be decided in twenty-four hours—perhaps it needed more deliberation or additional research— the staff member at least knew the issue had been brought to my attention and could truthfully explain to whoever awaited a decision that it was under consideration.[18]

Although oral communication is by far the biggest tool in the leader's communications toolbox, it is far from the only one. Leaders may be required to communicate in a variety of ways and should work to develop skill in all of them. All leaders are trainers to some degree and should be able to deliver a class or facilitate a discussion. Any leader may be called on to conduct a press briefing or conference and should be prepared to do so. All leaders will be required to submit written reports and to review the reports of those they work with. Their writing ability should reflect a measure of professionalism. Law enforcement leaders, at any level, may be required to speak before groups of citizens. Public speaking must be practiced to appear polished.

Skilled communication is a hallmark of a good leader. Great leaders strive to become adept at it. Listening, speaking, writing, and reviewing are all forms of communications in which a leader participates. The ability to do them well will distinguish the leader from his peers. Failure to do them well will mark him as incompetent and cost him the respect of his troops. Operationally, the costs can be even higher.

Particularly at the lower levels of supervision, face-to-face oral communication is part and parcel of operational briefings. When communications failures occur in an operational setting, the results can be disastrous. A couple of experiences with operational communications failures will illustrate this point clearly.

• • • • • • •

As a rookie officer, I was offered the opportunity to work as a part-time undercover. For a cop from my lily-white background, the chance to impersonate a crack dealer while helping to fight the war on drugs was about the most fun I could hope to have on the job. After a couple of years of regular sell-bust operations, my partners and I were comfortable and confident. During a normal operation, our team would routinely arrest several dealers in a row. When that portion of the operation was finished, my partner and I would replace the dealers on one corner and start targeting purchasers. We had never failed to net at least a couple of users.

On one of my last operations, things were not going well. It was a cold winter night. Foot traffic in our operation area was low. Even the crackheads were inside, trying to stay warm. We moved from corner to corner, trying to get something going. One of our well-known regulars approached us. If we got him, he was going to be my first "hat trick." He'd already bought from me and been arrested twice before. Tonight, however, he got spooked at the last second and walked away without making the buy. I was starting to get frustrated.

After several hours, with absolutely no takers, our backup called for a meet. Everyone was tired and cold. It was time to shut the operation down. I couldn't believe it. I'd never run a failed operation. Since my partner and I had driven a covert car into the area, then walked several blocks, we were going to have to walk back.

I told my backup that we were going to head back to the car. I also related the route we were going to take and suggested that if we stumbled across any opportunities on the way back, we would try to make a sale. I wasn't ready to give up yet.

As luck would have it, about halfway back to the car, we ran across a pretty heated argument. One guy was leaning into the driver's window of a car. There were at least two people in the car, and there was a lot of yelling back and forth. I couldn't tell for sure what was happening, but it didn't look good. We slowed down to get a better look. As we walked by, the car sped off. The guy who had been leaning in the window looked familiar. He was definitely a dealer.

I told my partner that I wanted to head out to the nearby main street. I just had a hunch. I told him to transmit over the wire that we were heading to a nearby intersection. Since I had told our backup that we were going to be looking for activity on the walk back to the car, I figured they would be able to hear us over the wire as they covered our extraction. He made the transmission, and we changed direction. As soon as we got to the intersection, the same car drove by. They looked us over, then pulled up and waved us down. I knew we were going get somebody that night.

I approached the male driver. He wanted to know what we had. As I was dealing with him, the female passenger was screaming that the other guy we had seen had just ripped them off. They really wanted to buy, but they wanted to try what we had before they made a deal. They weren't getting robbed again. My partner was at the rear of the car, trying to put a vehicle description and plate number out. Our backup was nowhere in sight. I needed to stall.

I decided to play on their paranoia. I told them that I'd show them the product but not on the side of the road. I told them to pull into a nearby parking lot and we'd meet them there. As we moved after them, my partner continued to transmit over the wire. Once in the parking lot, it would be easy for our backup team to box them in.

I moved to the driver's door. My partner moved to the rear of the car. I haggled over price and the size of the rocks. My partner continued to transmit over the wire. I let the driver examine the product. He wanted to sample it. I stayed in role and strung him along. The female passenger exited the car and came around to the driver's side. I kept haggling with both of them. Finally, I made the sale. There was still no sign of our backup. I gave the buy signal and my partner transmitted the buy.

I couldn't stand to let them drive away. I made a decision to break cover and make the arrest ourselves. I figured by the time we started screaming the arrest commands, our backup would figure out where we were, and we'd haul them off to jail. I signaled my partner, pulled out my badge, and drew my firearm.

As I heard myself screaming, "Police! Don't move!" I watched the female dive through the driver's window. The male slid over the seat and she ended up in the driver's seat. Everything went into slow motion. She moved to put the car in gear, but it slipped into reverse. I saw the vehicle moving toward my partner. I pushed my pistol's front sight onto the driver and kept screaming for her to stop. My partner started to move out of the way, and the driver slammed the car into drive. Suddenly, the car was headed at me. The next thing I knew, my arms were inside the car and I was caught on the side view mirror. This couldn't be happening.

I rolled off of the car and fell to the side. The car screamed out of the parking lot, and we took off running, screaming into the wire. Where the hell was our backup? We chased the car back to the inter-section and watched as it sped away. House lights started coming on, and I heard sirens heading our way. Perfect. I looked at my partner and told him to lie down, before our own guys shot us. Just perfect.

After the dust settled and we made it back to the station, we found out what had happened. Our backup units were never in the area. As soon as we started back to our car, they had gone right to the station. They never heard a single word we said and had no idea that we were in contact. The first indication they had of a problem in the operational area was when they heard the call dispatched for two black males with handguns chasing each other down the street. Since I had never requested a brief back when I discussed our exit plan with them, they just assumed we had walked to the car and driven back to the station. I learned a lot of valuable lessons that night. What I learned about the importance of clear operational communications was particularly important. Unfortunately, the lesson didn't stick as firmly as it could have.

• • • • • • •

Be-de-de-beep-Be-de-de-beep-Be-de-de-beep... One more time, normal life was interrupted by the incessant chirping of my team pager. I turned and looked at my wife, only to see the expected "What is it now?" expression on her face. I remember thinking to myself, "Well, at least it's warm and early," as I walked down the hall to find out what kind of crisis was going to ruin this suppertime. The tiny screen read, "Armed, barricaded subject," and gave the crisis location. I grabbed my badge and my gun and headed for the truck.

I drove directly to the station and was met by the on-duty senior team members. As they described the situation, I felt a sense of dread accompanied by déjà-vu. About nine years earlier, as a brand-new Special Response Team operator, I had responded to the same location. The subject, a mentally ill male with extreme paranoia, had threatened to harm a teacher. Our subject had engaged in past violent acts that had resulted in his firearms license being revoked and all of his guns being seized. Even though we had his guns, we knew he was an avid outdoorsman with access to bows, knives, and other antique weapons. He thought this teacher had mistreated his son and had threatened retalia-tion. Based on his past and the threats, the SRT was activated to take him into custody. The arrest wasn't pretty, but it was accomplished without injury to the suspect or officers. As we cuffed him and rolled him over, he looked up at the arrest team and said, "Wow, you guys are good. Can I join your team?" Now we were going to have to go get him again.

This time, the situation was more serious. According to the information we had, our old acquaintance had stopped taking his medication. This evening, something had set him off. The same son that had prompted his threats a decade ago had somehow offended him. Since his wife had managed to get his guns returned, he had grabbed a pistol and threatened to shoot the kid. The son had fled the house to escape his father's wrath. As the father started emptying the gun safe and strategically placing weapons throughout the house, his wife had grabbed their daughter, and they'd fled, too. She had contacted the police out of concern for her children.

Patrol officers had responded to the area, blocked off the street, and placed the house under surveillance. Investigators had interviewed the wife and daughter and were trying to locate the son. Supervisors had decided that given past history and all of the weapons involved, the SRT should be activated. This one wasn't going to go as smoothly as the last.

We responded to a preselected staging area that was close to the target house but offered ample security and space. Once in place, we organized an immediate action team (IAT) and assigned them to a vehicle for a quick response. While the IAT was developing their assault plan, the rest of us went to work on the rest of the plan. The negotiators arrived on scene and started working on an intelligence package so they'd have some background for their communications. We assigned four operators to a reconnaissance team. Since we had been told that patrol had placed the house under continuous surveillance at the outset of the call, we decided that the recon team could accomplish three missions. They could scout the approach routes for the rest of the team to follow them to the target. While they were en route, they could identify potential locations for a sniper/observer team to set up overwatch on the target. Finally, once they reached the target, they could establish an inner perimeter and take over surveillance from the patrol units.

I called the recon team over and briefed them on the three missions. Because security was critical and because we had not actually observed the target location, I told them that I wanted them to meet with the patrol unit closest to our location and have that officer lead them to the target area. We had been told that the patrol officers had actually identified the proper house by number, so they had the best information about where we were going. The recon team acknowledged their instructions and started out. This is when the operation took a decided turn for the worse.

With the recon team on their way, the rest of the command staff started working on a detailed plan. Our next order of business was to get our overwatch team into place. The snipers were preparing their equipment and waiting for the word that the recon team had located a suitable location for their perch. We were examining maps and photos of the area so that the snipers could pick a route that would put them across the street from the target unobserved. While I helped them plan their approach, the senior team leader was forming the deliberate assault team. The negotiators were identifying phone numbers to establish contact with the subject. Everything was proceeding normally. I was starting to feel that this operation would be resolved successfully.

Suddenly, the normal communications of the staging area were interrupted by a radio broadcast. The voice on the radio was the senior member of the recon team, and his tone was deceptively calm as he stated, "Shots fired. Shots fired. I am taking fire and am pinned down, unable to move. You'd better get someone up here quick."

His voice was so normal, that at first it didn't register. I remember looking at each of the other operators standing around me, waiting for one of them to tell me that I had imagined it, that I had misunderstood the transmission. Then, as fast as a thought, we jumped into the vehicles, screaming at each other to get moving. I don't remember much of the drive, even though I was driving. My first real recollection is lying in the street next to a sniper and setting up an improvised hide, behind a truck, hoping to cover our officers' withdrawal.

Things started happening really quickly. We linked up with the recon team and determined that no one was hit. The IAT brought a negotiator up to a position of cover in the neighboring yard, and he established contact with the subject by shouting through an open upstairs window. Before anyone really knew what was happening, the subject lay down his gun and, following the negotiator's surrender instructions, walked out into the waiting arms of the IAT. He was taken into custody and placed in a cruiser for transport. The entry team entered and cleared the house, then requested crime scene to come in and collect the guns that were scattered around the house. As the adrenaline levels plunged, we started asking questions. What had gone wrong? How had this happened?

As additional resources and upper-level command staff flooded into the area, we were able to discover some things. The first realization was that patrol officers had never actually placed the house under observation. Due to the geography of the neighborhood and the wide variety of weapons reported in the target, their observation positions allowed them to see only the driveway of the house. The second realization was that the driveway was between the target and the closest adjoining house. The third realization was that although the patrol officer at the far end of the street had identified the house while traveling to his post, the near officer hadn't actually observed it. He had received his information from the first officer and was orienting to the house based on that information. As I started asking more questions, I had a chance to speak to the members of the recon team. Although I had believed my instructions and requirements to be quite clear, there had been some confusion. When they reached the observation post, they had spoken to the officer and asked where the target was. He responded by pointing out the driveway. They thought he was indicating the house. They didn't ask him to lead them there.

As they made their approach, they were angling for the house that they thought was their last known point of cover and concealment. It was actually the target. As they split around the house to continue to the next house, the security light in the rear of the house went on. When it did, an officer near the front of the target was exposed as he sought cover behind a tree. The subject saw the movement and fired one round from a laser-equipped handgun through an upstairs window. Later investigation would show that he didn't actually fire at the officer but instead threw the round off into space. After firing the round, he continued to paint the tree with the laser, causing the officer to remain behind cover.

As the officers told me their story, I realized that I had neglected one of my earliest and most important lessons in communications. Communications isn't simply about delivering a message. It is about making sure that the message is received and understood. In tactical situations, we ensure this by using briefing talkbacks. Although I had told my recon team exactly where I wanted them to go and what I wanted them to do, in my haste, I had not asked them to repeat the instructions back to me. While I thought it was clear that I wanted someone who had already looked at the house to lead them to a suitable jump-off point, they thought I simply wanted the officer to show them the house. Had we engaged in a talkback, when they had gotten to the observation point and discovered that no one had actual eyes on the house, they could have radioed back their discovery. We would have modified the plan or developed a new one. Instead, to complete my directives, as they understood them, they proceeded with incomplete information. The end result could have been tragic on many levels. Instead, it was just embarrassing—and educational.

● ● ● ● ● ● ●

COURAGEOUS

Exemplary leaders display great personal courage. Normally, when we think of courage, we think of physical courage or bravery in the face of harm or death. Certainly, great military leaders and inspirational law enforcement leaders may have displayed physical courage. However, this is not the type of courage our employees pay the most attention to. Actually, physical courage is simply an extension of personal courage. Personal courage permeates all aspects of a successful leader's leadership style.

Colonel Danny McKnight, a bona fide hero who displayed great physical courage in Somalia, describes personal courage this way: It is "making the hard right decision, instead of the easy wrong one. The one that may not make you look good today, but will be the right one down the road."[19] For a leader, courage is not just about facing physical danger. Instead, it is about facing adversity and negativity and criticism and apathy from all sources. Whether it comes from the organization, from the bosses, from the troops, from the media, from the community, or anywhere else, a leader must confront it. Leaders make decisions not because they are easy but because they are right. Obviously, this requires a good ethical center and moral compass. However, as discussed earlier, we expect our leaders to behave ethically. Therefore, we are justified in expecting them to make the right decisions, even if they are difficult or controversial.

Personal courage requires leaders to understand a few important roles. They are obviously responsible for accomplishing the mission. They are also responsible for the health, well-being, education, and development of their troops. They are responsible for their relationship with their bosses. They are responsible for their duty to the community. Within the framework of these responsibilities, they must make courageous decisions that serve all their responsibilities equally. Many times, these decisions will be strategic, big-picture actions. They may not offer the immediate gratification that various parties to the decisions seek. Therefore, they may be unpopular or misunderstood. Leaders accept this and make the right decision anyway.

Once personal courage is developed, physical courage follows. In a dangerous situation, the courageous leader decides to act appropriately. She does this not because the action is heroic but because it is right. It is right for the troops, the mission, and the agency. It is right for a leader to display "courage under fire," whether that fire is literal or metaphorical. Any other decision undermines her role as a leader.

LOYAL

For a leader to be effective, loyalty is a critical character trait. We owe loyalty to many. One aspect of loyalty was discussed above—loyalty to those who are absent. We will examine other specific loyalties here.

Perhaps the most important but often overlooked form of loyalty is loyalty to our people. The value of this cannot be overemphasized. One of the most common misconceptions of newly promoted supervisors is the belief that the employees whom they supervise work for them (the supervisor). Let's examine this notion.

As a supervisor, your troops are producers. They actually perform the work, produce the product, make the cases, or whatever your desired end result is. They do that work for the organization. Good, bad, or otherwise, they would continue to do that work with or without you. They might not do it well, but they would do it, if for no other reason than their compensation is tied to that outcome.

You, the supervisor, have a responsibility to provide direction, guidance, and support. Your mission is to provide these to the producers. You receive direction from above and channel it to your people. Why? You do it so that they can do their jobs better. When you look at it this way, you really work for your people. Your job is to enable them to do theirs. You are their support staff. Since you work for them, you must remain loyal to them.

Loyalty to your people means that you will look out for their best interests. You will advocate for them with the rest of the chain of command. You seek the best training, education, equipment, and opportunities for them. You do this because they are *your* people and they deserve it. Loyalty to your people means that you will stand by them for as long as they deserve it. You will have enough faith in them to trust them to do their job. You will empower them to act as individuals, secure in the knowledge that they will act in the best interests of the organization. Loyalty to your people requires mutual trust and respect. According to Colonel McKnight, "If your subordinates know you respect them, they will do anything in the world for you to accomplish the mission."[20]

When subordinates begin to feel that you don't respect them or their abilities, it erodes their degree of respect for you. After a few years on the job as a patrol officer, I was fortunate to be selected to serve as a member of our Special Response Team. I was thrilled with the assignment and applied myself to my SRT duties with determination and vigor. Soon after I became a fully operational member of the SRT, our unit went from being a local team to being a regional team with countywide responsibilities. With the regionalization, we received a new set of written standard operating procedures (SOPs). Among the SOPs was a new policy titled the Emergency Rapid Deployment (ERD) policy.

Essentially, the ERD stated that if a law enforcement situation was deemed to be extraordinary and beyond the normal means of responding patrol officers, the commanding officer could deem it to be an ERD. In that case, all on-duty SRT members would respond to the scene, and upon arrival, the senior SRT member would assume tactical command. The SRT officer would remain in command until relieved by a senior or more qualified SRT member.

Today, in the era of the Incident Command System and National Incident Management System, the concept of an ERD policy probably doesn't appear that unusual. However, in a paramilitary organization prior to September 11, 2001, the ERD flew in the face of conventional wisdom. To give you an idea of how poorly the ERD was received, I'll share this story.

• • • • • • •

Shortly after the ERD was disseminated, my patrol shift commander called my team leader and me into his office. The shift commander was the senior lieutenant in the organization. We were both patrol officers. In most respects, he still considered me a rookie. When we arrived in his office, he pushed a copy of the ERD policy across his desk and asked if we had read it. We both stated that we had. He asked what we thought of it. We told him that we thought that it provided patrol supervisors with another tool to speed up deployments in a tactical situation and that it was intended to provide them with options. After we explained our perspective, he shared his. Essentially, he told us that as he read the ERD, if something went terribly wrong on his shift, he could turn the situation over to us and in the event that we couldn't resolve it, he could then blame us for the failure. It wasn't a conversation destined to inspire confidence and respect in my commander. It did, however, clearly let me know what I could expect from him. He clearly didn't respect us or our training and abilities. I certainly lost a large measure of respect for him. I wasn't likely ever to forget that conversation.

As a supervisor, you must also be loyal to your organization. Any midlevel manager who is heard constantly beating up on the agency will not be viewed as very professional. This is not to say that you must agree with or be happy with everything your agency does. You can disagree, express displeasure, and work for changes. However, when you talk about the agency, particularly to the public, emphasize the positives. Display your pride and confidence in the organization. This doesn't mean that you have to be untruthful. Emphasize what your agency does well, address what needs improvement, and follow that up with changes that are in progress or suggestions.

Loyalty to your organization also requires that you adhere to your agency's vision, mission, and values. Do you have a written vision statement, mission statement, and value statement? If so, do you know what they are? Do you take them into consideration when making decisions?

Loyalty to your organization may sometimes come into conflict with loyalty to your people. However, the two must not be allowed to interfere with one another. When decisions are being made, advocate for your workers. Look out for their best interests. If the decision will have a negative impact on your troops, express your displeasure. However, once the decision is made, carry it out to the best of your ability. Explain it to your troops with regard to the benefit to the organization. Be a loyal follower and advocate for the decision. Never place yourself at odds with the organization by saying that your people have to do this because "they" (the administration) say so. Just as you are an advocate for your people with the administration, so must you be an advocate for the administration with your people.

Leaders must also be loyal to their individual bosses. You may not personally like your boss. You may not agree with everything he does or says. However, he is your boss, and you owe him a professional measure of loyalty. It is not enough to be loyal to a boss. To be an effective leader, you must display active loyalty to your superiors. You must make it known that you will do the best you can to support your current administration. Establish yourself as a loyal follower.

Leaders who are not seen as being loyal followers may be viewed as subversives. If your troops come to regard you as someone who works toward your own agenda rather than that of the agency or administration, what will happen when you are the boss? Will your troops then regard it as acceptable to work contrary to your goals and aims? If you do not want your followers to sabotage your efforts, you must not be seen as sabotaging those of your boss. The best way to do this is to be a loyal follower.

Sometimes, becoming a loyal follower may require a direct approach. Over the course of my law enforcement career, I have had one supervisor who has been a very active advocate of my professional development. After several years of having this person support and promote my training and education, I began to detect a pulling back. I quickly realized that he had stopped regarding me as a student and started regarding me as competition. The only way to repair the mentoring relationship was to tell him that as ambitious as I might be, I had no interest in his job as long as he was with the agency. Once he left, it might be a different story, but as long as he remained with our department, it was my intention to support his efforts with my best efforts. Did my reassurances work? I think so. After that conversation, our relationship was as positive as ever. He continued to support me in advancing my career, and I continued to support his efforts and actions within the department. The positive interaction continues to this day.

• • • • • • •

EXEMPLARY

The best leaders lead by example. People often hear the expressions "lead by example" and "leading from the front" and think they are the same thing. They are very similar but not identical.

Leading by example requires a high level of professionalism. It requires both the competence and confidence discussed previously. During one of his presentations, Colonel Danny McKnight related the story of his change of command ceremony upon taking command of the 3rd Ranger Battalion. After the outgoing commanding officer made his farewell speech, Colonel McKnight addressed his battalion. He stood before them and simply stated that he would never ask anything of them that he wasn't willing to do with them. Basically, he left it at that.

Having made that statement, McKnight had to lend credence to it. He chose to do this by taking physical training (PT) with his troops every day and making airborne jumps with them whenever possible. According to McKnight, every morning when he approached a unit to join them for PT, he could hear the young Rangers mumbling. He claims that he knew that they were saying, "Here comes the old man. Let's see if *we* can kill him today!"[21] McKnight started PT with his units and finished with them every day. In this way, his men could see his willingness to do what he required of them.

Despite this relationship with his troops, in Somalia, Colonel McKnight was not at the front of a Ranger "chalk," manning a machine gun or driving a Humvee. He was a little ways back, coordinating movements and communications. Having previously led by example, it was not always necessary to lead from the front. His role and duties required a larger view of the situation than he could get from the front lines. He had subordinate officers and sergeants to lead from the front. However, he was right there with his Rangers in the middle of that battle. While performing his command responsibilities, he continued to lead by example.

Leading by example is necessary all of the time. Leading from the front may be required only of small-unit leaders during an actual crisis. Leading by example is how leaders set the standard that will be expected at the front during the crisis, and it applies to all areas of organizational interest.

When leadership by example and leadership from the front are not clearly distinguished, the resulting confusion can have a dramatic effect on operations. An example from another SRT callout may illustrate this confusion.

• • • • • • •

It was a hot summer day in New England. Although I had been an SRT team leader for a couple of years, my brand-new sergeant's stripes validated my position on the team. As an SRT team sergeant, I had the responsibility for leading operators into tactical situations and finding a successful resolution. I regarded it as my job to provide my chief and his command staff with a variety of options and to slow down situations until those options had been implemented.

The previous evening, the entire team had been involved in performing a variety of public relations demonstrations as part of a citywide community policing program. After finishing the demos, I had gone into work and completed my overnight midnight shift. Following that, I had gone home and climbed into bed, completely exhausted. Approximately eight hours later, the sound that awoke me wasn't my alarm clock. Instead, it was the insistent chirp of my pager, signaling a callout.

I rolled out of bed and checked the tiny screen. All it provided was a location and the brief description "Armed, barricaded subject." I called into the station and was instructed to proceed directly to the scene. Other officers were bringing our equipment from the station, and the tactical response needed to be coordinated. I pulled on the same tactical uniform I had worn the night before and headed out. While driving, I called in again for more information.

Patrol officers had responded to a call of an individual threatening to do harm to himself. When they got there, they found the apartment open and entered in an attempt to contact the subject. While proceeding through the apartment, they were hailed by the subject. He told them that he was in the attic and was armed. He told them that he would shoot anyone who came up after him. The officers sensibly backed out of the apartment and called for help. SRT was the help they were looking for. As a team leader, I knew that any on-duty team members would have requested ERD authority and attempted to coordinate an Immediate Action Plan. My job on arrival would be to coordinate with the on-scene commanders, check the deployment of any SRT members, redeploy them if necessary, lock down the perimeter, and start developing some plans.

I arrived at the target area 15 minutes after my pager had sounded. As I pulled up to the target, I observed that the entire street was shut down. That was good. I saw a patrol officer standing in the roadway. I pulled up to him to find out where the target, the staging area, and the command post were located. His answer to my first question was the first indication that maybe the situation wasn't what I had thought. He pointed over his shoulder at the duplex he was standing in front of and said, "Right there!" From my truck, I could clearly see windows on all three levels of the target, facing the street. There was a guy with a gun in there. I suggested that he find some cover and drove deeper into the scene to get out of the line of fire.

At the opposite end of the scene, I saw the command vehicle and the team truck. As I exited my truck, I asked an officer where I could find the scene commanders. I needed to coordinate our arrival with them. The answer I got was a little distressing. According to the officer, the two senior supervisors were in the target. I was confused. If they were inside the target, then who was running the overall scene? We needed to establish a perimeter, designate a command post, develop an immediate action plan, coordinate additional arriving units, prepare for the arrival of the media, and perform dozens of additional tasks. These were established protocols for a barricaded subject.

I already knew that I had officers standing in the hot zone, and hadn't seen any obvious signs of an inner perimeter. I thought that the best thing that I could do to facilitate the operation was to relieve the brass inside the target and let them resume command. I went to the team truck to grab my vest, helmet, and rifle. As I charged my rifle, I heard a shout. A detective yelled to me that they wanted me inside. I took off running. As I crossed the street, shots rang out. I entered the target and charged up the stairs. When I entered the attic, the suspect was down. One of my teammates was administering first aid. Someone handed me a shotgun. The radio buzzed with constant chatter. What had happened?

As I took stock of the situation, I realized something: the senior supervisors on scene were all in this room. As soon as the subject was transported, all of the officers who had been inside were removed from the scene. Since the senior officers had been inside, they were all isolated.

By default, I was momentarily left as senior on the scene. My fellow team sergeant arrived on scene during the height of activity. The irony became quickly apparent. Two first-line tactical supervisors were attempting to manage a critical incident on behalf of the department. The senior supervisors were removed due to their having been present during the shooting. Our chief and senior captain arrived shortly thereafter and took overall responsibility for the scene. That allowed us to focus on specific tasks and missions. For the rest of the night, I found myself asking, "How had our roles become reversed? What was the leadership lesson?"

It was many years before I realized that "lead from the front" could be misconstrued. Only after discussing the above callout with

Colonel McKnight did I realize that sometimes, being with your troops in the thick of it may not be the best place for you to be.

· · · · · · ·

Do you expect your subordinates to behave a certain way, speak a certain way, or carry themselves a certain way? Do you have expectations of acceptable language and conduct? Does your department have standards for uniform and personal appearance? Do you expect a certain amount of responsibility and decorum from your people while off duty? The only way to make these expectations a reality is to model the desired behaviors and conduct for your people. This requires leaders to be role models. Expecting one behavior and modeling another is insincere and will cause your people to doubt your sincerity. We all know how we felt as children when our parents, teachers, or other adults told us to "do as I say, not as I do." Your people will feel the same way if you don't set the example for them to follow.

PASSIONATE

The best leaders are passionate about their profession and their leadership role. They regard what they do as a calling and they communicate their love of the job to those around them. Their passion is infectious. For law enforcement leaders, this can become very important.

Law enforcement is a difficult career. Its practitioners face a wide variety of pressures from a wide variety of sources. Under these pressures, it is easy for us to lose our motivation. It falls on the leader to overcome this loss. Highly successful leaders do not labor under the misconception that they can externally motivate their employees. Motivation is an internal drive. Leaders recognize, however, that they can remind their troops of what originally motivated them. Through his own passion, the leader can communicate the love of the mission, the desire for action, and the sense of service that young officers felt when they first signed up. By communicating this passion, leaders can inspire their people to rekindle their own motivations.

• • • • • • •

In 2007, I was promoted to the rank of acting captain and was transferred from Operations to Administration. Although the transfer involved a move into areas of responsibility that were in most cases completely foreign to me, I retained responsibility for training. I was happy to keep the training assignment, because training really had been the key to success in my career. It was through a variety of training assignments and associations that I had been able to rise through the ranks and reach this point. I love being a cop, but being a law enforcement trainer has truly become a passion.

Even though I retained training responsibility, actually participating in training was going to be a bit of a challenge. My schedule changed, so it no longer coincided with our normal in-service schedule. Additionally, for the first time in my career, my day-to-day uniform was business attire. That wasn't exactly conducive to hands-on training.

Shortly after moving into the administrative assignment, I had the opportunity to attend a morning in-service block. They were short one instructor, but the topic wasn't overly involved. I watched for a couple of minutes and realized that the class would go a little more smoothly with an additional instructor. I removed my sport coat, cleared my weapon, and jumped into the class. I didn't really think that much about it. One of my instructors needed some help, and I was in a position to provide it. Over the period of the next several months, I had the opportunity to repeat this scene. I loved it. Not only was I responsible for training, I was down in the dirt, doing training. It was awesome.

Several months later, my chief announced that he was leaving our agency to move to a different chief's job. The process of seeking a temporary agency head started. It wasn't until this process started that I realized what an impact my conducting training had on our troops. During the interview and selection process, one of the statements offered was that I "was a captain's captain" and that I was really concerned about the welfare of my troops. While that was true, I hadn't given it any thought. I was a trainer, with a passion for sharing information and knowledge with my people. That passion had clearly been communicated within our organization.

• • • • • • •

Not only are leaders passionate about their chosen field with their colleagues, they are passionate about it with anyone who will listen. Over the course of my career, I have had the opportunity to meet and interact with a large variety of police professionals from local, state, federal, and international police agencies. Nearly every one of them has expressed the same sentiment to me: law enforcement is the world's greatest career, and if they had to choose over again, they would still choose law enforcement. Since my experience is largely restricted to law enforcement, that is the only field I can personally speak to. However, I would hazard to guess that professionals and leaders in every field would express the same passion. When my agency affords me the opportunity to address groups of citizens, I remind them that my officers are members of a noble profession and that they choose to be there. I tell them of my officers' performances and accomplishments. If I can share just a small portion of my passion for my job with a citizen group, I will have made a difference.

CHAPTER 4

PERSONAL DEVELOPMENT

"Leadership is when other people do what you want them to
do, because they want to do it."

—General Dwight Eisenhower

General Eisenhower's quote defines our role as leaders simply but begs
the question "How do we make them want to do it?" The answer lies
in a variety of skills, and those skills need to be acquired through
study, experience, and practice. Despite the old adage, great leaders
are not born. They are not even simply made. Great leaders are crafted
and developed carefully, skillfully, and over time. Sometimes, they
are crafted by mentors or organizations that require their leadership.
Often, however, they craft themselves. This process of crafting a leader,
manager, or executive is referred to in the trade as "development."

Professor Alec Horniman of the University of Virginia describes
the critical difference between training and development during his
discussions with the Executive Development Institute. According to

Professor Horniman, if you train somebody to do something, when they leave the class, they should be able to perform the behavior or task. Trained behavior is measurable and testable. Development, on the other hand, is fluid. It is nebulous. During a development program, course leaders facilitate discussion. They present theories and options in hopes of expanding the participants' perspective. However, it is up to the individual participant to take that information and apply it to his particular circumstances or environment. In discussions, Horniman explains why he believes that leading and learning are inextricably linked. He defines learning as "doing differently with what we know." Recognizing this is part of the development process. While we can train knowledge, we develop learning. Leading is also "doing differently." This is one of the reasons that we must "learn to lead."

With this distinction in mind, we can see that leadership cannot really be trained. No one can sit you in an in-service classroom and say that at the end of this x-hour block of instruction, you will be a "leader." Instead, leaders are developed. The development process can only succeed if the individual is receptive to development and if development opportunities are afforded to her. Having made someone a leader, by virtue of conferring rank or position on her, how can we be sure that she is exercising leadership? We need to develop our leaders fully. However, what particular skills are we hoping to improve through development? Answering this question is challenging. In its academy lesson "Organizational Leadership," the DEA lists six skill sets that, taken in combination, can describe leadership. These six skill sets, originally described by the Blanchard Institute, are subsets of what it is to be a leader. Each can be improved through executive development.

TECHNICAL SKILL

The study of technical skills goes back to our discussion of competence and confidence. Many technical skills are trainable. In law enforcement, these include physical skills like controlling and apprehending, shooting, and driving. They also include skills like writing, reporting, processing, and handling evidence. With respect to leadership, technical skills include some things that cannot be trained easily, like public speaking, delivering a press briefing, or running a critical incident. You can learn the elements in a classroom, but competency must be developed with practice. Some of this can be done in training through simulation, but much of the time, it will come with experience and being mentored by a more senior leader. The importance of developing technical skills cannot be overrated. Technical expertise is essential to earning and establishing credibility.

INTERPERSONAL SKILL

Of all the leadership skill sets, interpersonal skills may be the most difficult to master. However, they are the most important. No one, regardless of his skills, knowledge, and abilities, can lead if he cannot influence other people. The ability to communicate with and relate with others is a basic necessity of leadership. Although it is possible to manage people and programs without good interpersonal skills, it is not possible to lead them. Leadership is rooted in personal interaction.

We have discussed many aspects of interpersonal skills elsewhere. Interpersonal skills involve the ability to communicate with, listen to, and care about your people. They enable you to provide support to your troops and to counsel and coach them regarding professional and personal issues.

Interpersonal skills are the foundation of effective leadership. Fortunately, they can be improved with training, development, and time. Those of us who choose to become leaders must choose to become better at interacting with our troops.

Having good interpersonal skills does not mean that a leader must always be kind or nice. Effective discipline also requires the ability to communicate and listen effectively. Although the message may be unwelcome or unpleasant, it must be delivered effectively. Communicating the full meaning requires sound interpersonal skills.

PROGRAM SKILL

Perhaps the most difficult of the skill sets to understand is program skill. Essentially, program skill is the ability of a leader to turn a vague concept into a workable program. In today's world of community policing, the ability of leaders to design and implement programs is essential. It is important to recognize that program skill is not the ability to manage an existing program. Any able manager can take a written program and replicate it or implement it. Instead, program skill is found in the leader who first develops the program.

Leaders with program skill can recognize a problem, brainstorm potential solutions, and wade through the husks and the chaff of the brainstorming session until a few valuable kernels emerge. These leaders will take those kernels, plant them, and cultivate and nurture them until an operational program is born. They see that program through to its conclusion, modifying and adapting it as necessary. Finally, they assess the results and move on to the next problem and program.

As law enforcement practitioners, we are accustomed to receiving a program description, studying it, and copying the implementation phase of that program. By developing program skill in our leaders, however, agencies can write their own custom programs to meet their problems. This is not to say that agencies must reinvent the wheel. Researching and comparison shopping is always wise. However, by utilizing program skill, instead of picking one generic program, leaders can select the best elements of several to combine into their own new creation.

POLITICAL SKILL

Of the six skill sets that we are examining here, perhaps the least appreciated and most distasteful to discuss is political skill. In our time, the words *political* and *politics* often carry a negative connotation. This is largely owing to our past experiences with our politicians. Unfortunately, this connotation causes us to look with suspicion on anything that is associated with the terms. The actual definition of *politic* is "characterized by shrewdness in managing, contriving, or dealing; sagacious in promoting a policy; shrewdly tactful."[22] Since being shrewd or wise is not, in and of itself, negative, neither is politics. In essence, being "political" is having the ability to manage and get things done by being astute and knowledgeable. Only when accompanied by deceit or a lack of fundamental ethics does *politics* become a dirty word.

The definition of political skill utilized by the DEA is as follows: "The ability to know where power exists in an organization and how to access that power to get your program accomplished."

While this definition itself is subject to a negative interpretation, let us recognize that nothing in the definition suggests unethical behavior. Instead, it indicates that we should be aware of our situation and our organization. By being fully aware of what is happening in an organization, we know where the sources of power in that organization are. Having recognized the sources of power, we can determine what is necessary to tap into that power and get things done. If we decide that what is necessary is negative or unethical behavior, we will be labeled as "political." If we decide to remain positive and ethical, most people would not associate our behavior with politics. Instead we may be labeled an "astute power broker." However, our activity still shows political astuteness.

A leader who recognizes the value of political skill assiduously examines his organization and cultivates relationships with everyone who can influence the outcomes of programs. In most organizations, this automatically includes senior executives. In police organizations, this could also include the leaders of the union or association. It could include police commissions or advisory groups. It might also include neighborhood watch organizations, citizen groups, or nonprofits. Each of these groups and many more are potential sources of power in particular instances. Political skill is the ability to access power from the appropriate source and put it to work for the benefit of your organizational goals. This is not distasteful. It is simply informed leadership.

VISIONARY SKILL

With visionary skill, a supervisor can display true leadership. Without it, the supervisor is stuck in the realm of management. Visionary skill is the mark of a big-picture thinker. The definition of visionary skill is "the ability to see the organization as a whole entity, and to understand where the organization needs to go. The ability to look at the external environment and make changes to the internal environment."[23]

A leader who possesses visionary skill has the ability to recognize all of the components that make up the agency. She also has the ability to see how her agency fits into its specific community. Not only does the leader recognize the agency as it is today, she also recognizes where it must be in the future. The leader bases this future vision on factors both internal and external to the organization. The basis of visionary skill is competency in change. The importance of change will be discussed in detail in Chapter 8, "Change and Creative Thinking." However, visionary leaders recognize that change is not just useful but necessary.

Visionary leaders examine all aspects of their organizations. In police organizations, this means focusing not just on the obvious areas, such as personnel, policies, training, and equipment. They also focus on areas that are traditionally underregarded. These may include things like relations with the media, modifying and updating the agency's mission, changes and improvements in technology, and improved recruiting. Visionary leaders are not content to lead the current organization. Their goal is to lead the organization to a better future.

Lastly, visionary leaders understand one important concept and communicate this concept to their followers. They recognize that the behavior of each member of the organization reflects on the organization as a whole. What one member says or does is attributed to the entire organization. Likewise, the reputation of the organization reflects on both the community it serves and the entire profession. This is painfully apparent in law enforcement. A community whose police department or sheriff's office has a tarnished reputation may be viewed as unsafe. When one police department is racked with scandal, the entire profession suffers.

LINCHPIN CONCEPT

The last of the six subsets is not actually a skill at all. It is, instead, the recognition of a fundamental principle. Unfortunately, in many agencies, this principle goes unrecognized. Essentially, the linchpin concept states that the first-level supervisors of any organization are what tie the organization together. They are the linchpins. They are responsible for the organization's internal communication. They allow the command staff to know what is happening at the delivery-of-service level and vice versa. In the law enforcement community, this concept is typically summed up in the assertion that sergeants are the most important leadership level in any organization. Unfortunately, this assertion often receives more lip service than implementation.

According to the Blanchard Institute materials utilized by the DEA, the linchpin concept occurs only at the nexus of formal positions of leadership. I think that this framework fails to consider the realities of a leadership void. If an organization's first-level supervisors do not perform their linchpin duties, somebody else will. Who that somebody else is will be vitally important to an organization's success.

If an agency plays lip service to the importance of its first-level supervisors but doesn't empower them to perform their linchpin duties, communications failures will result. For example, senior officers may fail to recognize performance or morale issues with their troops. Misunderstandings and misconceptions will dramatically impact the agency's ability to perform its mission and deliver services.

Conversely, if the first-line supervisors do not recognize the importance of their role as linchpins, they may fail to carry out this important duty. As a result, their troops will find another way to enable communication. If the agency is generally healthy, the linchpin responsibilities may end up being performed by senior officers or officers who have earned a reputation as performers. These officers may have the trust and the ear of senior leaders. In this case, chain-of-command failures and resentment from the sergeants may result. If the agency is dysfunctional, the officers may come to rely on the rumor mill as their preferred method of communication. When this occurs, the agency is on the verge of a very slippery slope. The inevitable decline of the agency will eventually culminate in personnel at all levels feeling disenfranchised and out of touch with the goals and mission of the agency.

Recognizing and fostering the linchpin concept is essential to the health and success of any organization. Leaders at all levels must recognize their roles in this system. Senior executives must recognize the importance of their first-level supervisors and both rely on them and empower them to facilitate internal communication. More importantly, first-level supervisors must recognize and embrace their duty to facilitate communication between their troops and their senior officers. They must not only fulfill it but insist on it. First-level supervisors must solicit input from their troops and channel that information to upper-level management. They must also receive information from the upper levels, distill it into a message that will resonate with the troops, and pass it on. First-level supervisors must recognize that the success of their organization rests on their ability to successfully perform this task.

STAFF SKILL

Another skill set, which is not included in those utilized by the DEA, is important to a new leader. Even as a new supervisor, leaders must recognize the importance of staff skills. These skills, not operational in nature, are often overlooked, particularly by police supervisors. As police officers, we pride ourselves on our operational abilities. Once promoted, this predisposition follows through into our supervisory mind-set. While we readily recognize that we must be able to control a scene, coordinate an investigation, or lead a raid, we fail to recognize that none of these is possible without attention to administrative details.

Most first-level supervisors do not have to concern themselves overly with staff matters. However, those that are most effective and who see their careers advance recognize that an understanding of staff matters is critical. Consequently, they seek opportunities to cross-train in those skills. They recognize that an understanding of staffing, budgeting, recruiting, training, and other staff responsibilities will make them a better leader.

Although they might not have to perform these duties, operational leaders rely on staff members to provide them with the bodies, policies, and finances to carry out their tasks. An understanding of staff skills allows a leader to better appreciate their role in the organization. It enables him to see where his troops fit into the organization and how they interact with the other units. Understanding and learning how to perform staff skills allows new leaders to appreciate better some of the concerns and actions of their superior officers. Finally, learning to perform staff skills makes it possible for new leaders to become senior leaders in the future.

Having identified these critical areas that are suitable for development, we might ask, "Why is this important?" Any worker who wants to advance his career or his field must recognize that what is good enough for today will not be good enough for tomorrow. Personal development is the method we use to ensure that we continue to be effective and valuable contributors to our organization and our profession. As Stephen Covey so aptly states,

> Our most important financial asset is our own capacity to learn. If we don't continually invest in improving our own PC [production capability], we severely limit our options. We're locked into our present situation, running scared of our corporation or our boss's opinion of us, economically dependent and defensive.[24]

CHAPTER 5

VISION

> One of the fundamental problems in organizations, including families, is that people are not committed to the determinations of other people for their lives. They simply don't buy into them.... No involvement, no commitment.[25]
>
> —Stephen Covey, *The Seven Habits of Highly Effective People*

> A leader tries to link the past with the present and project the future. We have to gain something from where we have been.[26]
>
> —Mr. Jim Getty as President Abraham Lincoln, Presentation to the Drug Unit Commanders Academy, DEA Justice Training Center April 14, 2004

Vision has been referred to in both Chapter 1, "Management Versus Leadership" and Chapter 4, "Personal Development." These tangential references emphasized the importance of vision but didn't cover it adequately. Vision is one of the defining characteristics of a successful leader. Covey describes a leader as one who recognizes that his organization is in the wrong jungle. The discussion of visionary skill pointed out that a successful leader understands where his organization exists in relation to the greater community and where it is going.

To get more specific about both of these, it is necessary to dedicate some time to the idea of vision.

A truly visionary leader doesn't just recognize the "wrong jungle." To be truly visionary, a leader must work to create the right jungle. Any discussion of vision must begin with the idea of creating a vision. Generally, in leadership texts and classes, vision is the purview of senior leaders and chief executives. It is their responsibility to create a vision for the entire organization. However, leaders at every level can practice vision creation. As a sergeant, do I have a vision for my squad, my unit, or my team? If I do not, then how can I possibly evaluate where we are going?

How do we go about creating a vision? We begin with the realization that no matter how good our agency is, there is room for improvement. We then have to recognize that seeking improvement is not a condemnation of our current state or our past. It is not a "dig" at our current bosses. Seeking improvement is seeking excellence. By committing to continuous improvement, we seek to make our agency the best agency it can be. This is a worthy goal for any leader.

Once we acknowledge that there is room for improvement, it is necessary to perform some form of assessment of the agency. Whether we conduct formal surveys and assessment instruments designed to document the current state of our organization or we utilize informal methods of obtaining information, we must define the current state of our agency. Among the areas that we might consider are these: What is our mission? What are our values? What is our current level of service? Do we value our employees? What is our relationship with the community? Do we place enough emphasis on training and education? Do we encourage creative thinking? Do we reward appropriate behavior? There are hundreds, if not thousands, of other questions that might be asked. The point is to determine where we are today. If we don't recognize where we are today, we have no hope of getting where we want to go.

Having decided that there is room for improvement, the next step is to craft the vision that we seek. For chief executives, this will be a broad, wide-ranging concept that impacts the entire agency. For more junior leaders, it will be a narrower, more focused image of the unit's future. Once we have determined the scope of our vision, we have to start formulating it. This part of creating a vision carries two serious pitfalls. The first is determining whose vision it is. The second is a question of specificity. Let us examine each of these problems individually.

As leaders, we have decided to create a vision for our organization. Since we are the leaders, this responsibility falls upon us ... or does it? If we unilaterally decide what direction to take the agency, how will we move the agency there? We can't do it alone. If we don't include our people in the creation of the vision, they have no investment in its accomplishment. The vision is ours, but the task of achieving it is theirs. If they don't share our vision, they may not be interested in accomplishing it. As leaders, our job is to formulate broad outcomes and goals. However, we must solicit input from our troops to define the goals. The process relies on our including our troops, in-corporating their suggestions and concerns, earning their support and buy-in, and selling the value of the vision to each of them. Only if they agree with the vision will they be committed to accomplishing it, and their commitment is essential. During this phase, a leader's skills as a communicator and salesperson are put to the test. The vision must belong to the entire organization, not just to those appointed at the top.

My current organization has a vision statement. It was crafted in 1999 and rolled out in 2000 as a benchmark for our agency. It was meant to define where we wanted to go in the new millennium. To the credit of my chief and our command staff, they included members of the agency in the creation of the vision. They formed a committee consisting of all ranks and classifications of employees. They brought in an outside consultant to facilitate the process. They encouraged suggestions from the troops and included them. The result was this:

> The [Department] will be a professional, community-oriented police organization, providing quality service and performing in an effective, efficient, and courteous manner.

While this may appear to be a worthy vision, the problem is one of specifics. While we may have made some progress toward this vision, how will we know when we've achieved it? There are no standards of measurement or achievement. For our vision to be valuable, it must be attainable and measurable. If we've created an attainable and measurable vision, it must then be tracked to recognize accomplishment or failure and modified to provide new vision in the future. Many organizations create vision with a specific timetable: one quarter, six months, one year, etc.

Using the above example of a vision statement, how could we make it attainable, measurable and trackable? Let's try one possibility:

> In the next 12 months, this agency will increase its level of professionalism. For our purposes, increased professionalism will be a function of training, networking, and personal development. Each member of the organization will attend 40 hours of in-service training and one specialty course. Each member will attend one professional seminar or conference to increase the number of their professional acquain-

tances. Each member will subscribe to one professional publication or join one professional association.

In the next 12 months, this agency will increase its commitment to community policing. This will be accomplished by increasing the number of citizens involved in existing programs by 10 percent and increasing our number of community partnerships or programs by two.

In the next 12 months, this agency will increase quality of service by reducing service-related complaints by 10 percent.

In the next 12 months, this agency will increase its commitment to courteous service. We will achieve this by reducing citizen complaints about lack of courtesy by 25 percent.

Each of the above four vision statements is specific in time and desired outcome. We have ignored the goals of efficiency and effectiveness, not because they aren't important but because they are not specifically measurable by most line troops. For the other four visions, we not only know where we want to be, we know when we want to be there and how we will know when we have or haven't arrived. At the end of 12 months, we can evaluate each of these four visions. Depending on our successes, we can continue with these, modify them, or create new visions for the next period of time.

The above examples are agencywide visions. How can we apply this approach to lower-level leaders and smaller units? We can apply the same concept to a smaller scope and time frame. For example, as a sergeant, I might lay out the following vision for my squad:

In the next six months, this squad will reduce the number of officer injuries resulting from arrest situations. We will accomplish this by conducting ongoing training in the use of OC spray, batons, and handcuffs. We will adopt one consistent procedure for performing Standing Compliant Handcuffing. Every member of the squad will be responsible for complying with this procedure.

I might also focus on something other than job-specific performance:

> In the next quarter, this squad will increase the level of teamwork and commitment between members. We will accomplish this by conducting one squadwide, off-duty activity for members and their families.

These sample visions do not deal with broad, agencywide concerns. Instead, they are goals that will have the desired result of improving performance and attitude among members of a small unit. Every member of the unit can have a hand in crafting these smaller visions. If every small unit leader implemented a couple of small visions at a time, the eventual benefit to the entire agency would be enormous. Paired with the larger shiftwide and agencywide visions, this is a recipe for incredible change across the board.

Having crafted a vision, how do we make it work for us? One very effective way is to use our vision as kind of a road map for success. When we review a report, issue a press release, or write an operations plan, we can evaluate it in relation to our agency's vision. Was our behavior or performance consistent with our stated vision? Have we planned and acted in accordance with our principles? Are we making progress toward accomplishing our vision by carrying out these activities? If not, how can we make changes to be more consistent with our vision? Is there a training opportunity here? Can we see a chance to improve a policy? By utilizing our stated vision this way, every enforcement activity and administrative change becomes part of our continuous improvement. Employing vision in this way is a commitment to excellence.

Recognizing and embracing the importance of vision is perhaps the most important part of the process. Many agencies, including several with which I have been associated, suffer from lack of vision.

These are the agencies that define themselves by the expressions "We've always done it this way," and "If it isn't broken, why fix it?" Remember, vision is a fundamental aspect of leadership. Your troops expect it of you. Fail to provide them with one, and they will invent one of their own. If they are left to their own devices, their vision and yours likely will not correspond. Having decided to create our vision, we must include all our people in the process. We must also encourage leaders at all levels to engage in their own vision creation. Once committed to this process, we have set the stage for moving our agencies forward toward a new and hopefully better future.

CHAPTER 6

RISK

The next consideration for new leaders is the concept of risk. Any discussion of risk begins with a certain level of discomfort. As human beings, risk is not something that we readily embrace. We all recognize a risk when we experience one. *Risk* is peril, or something with potential for injury or loss. The dictionary defines *risk* as "someone or something that creates or suggests a hazard."[27] Even when we recognize a risk, we may not know how to respond to it. The decision we make when confronted with a risk plays a large part in whether we choose to manage or lead.

Having recognized a risk, what can we do? What are our choices? There really are not that many possibilities. Having recognized a risk, we can avoid it, ignore it, mitigate it, or manage it. Avoiding risk is an easy concept—having recognized the risk, we choose a course of action that will not require us to deal with it. Ignoring risk can be either a conscious choice or a cowardly response to panic. When we ignore risk, we allow ourselves to assume that the perceived hazard will not impact us. We choose to rely on luck instead of skill. Unfortunately for many of us in law enforcement, ignoring risk is a common behavior by police officers at all levels.

Mitigating risk is a little more complicated. By choosing to miti- gate risk, we acknowledge the potential loss or injury. However, once we've recognized it, we accept that some loss or injury is inevitable and take steps to minimize the amount suffered. Risk management may appear similar to mitigation. However, where mitigation accepts some loss as inevitable, risk management focuses on preventing loss. Risk management is an ongoing process. It is intended to help an agency move forward by focusing on possible outcomes and changing those outcomes to have the most beneficial impact on the organization.

The discussion of risk is another opportunity to explore the differ- ences between managers and leaders. All of us, especially those of us in law enforcement, are familiar with the effects of risk avoidance strate- gies. Many of our agency policies and procedures are written with the goal of risk avoidance in mind. It is important to recognize that the process of risk avoidance is a management technique. When managers are dedicated to maintaining the status quo and increasing efficiency, they benefit from risk avoidance. Managers incorporate strategies that will prevent loss or injury to the larger organization. Leaders, on the other hand, embrace a philosophy of risk management. They recog- nize that some risks, frequently referred to as "calculated risks," make progress possible. Leaders seek to make risk work for them.

Gordon Graham is an internationally recognized instructor on the concept of risk management. As an experienced law enforcement officer, attorney, and systems engineer, Captain Graham brings a unique perspective to the concept of risk. He is fond of repeating this simple phrase to his classes which sums up his teachings: "If it is predictable, it is preventable."

According to Captain Graham, if you don't accept some risk, progress is impossible. The key is to approach risk from a proactive point of view. Having recognized a risk, the next step is to determine its potential outcomes. After predicting the potential outcomes, we can take steps and implement systems to prevent them. We don't avoid the risk. We also don't simply accept some losses due to the risk and take steps to minimize them. Instead, we proactively make decisions and put systems in place to prevent those outcomes. We don't run from the risk, we don't ignore the risk, and we don't attempt to hold the risk at bay with barriers. Instead, we acknowledge the risk and work around it with different strategies that will prevent undesirable outcomes but still allow us to capitalize on advantageous outcomes.

Risk management allows agencies to move forward and make changes without being hamstrung by fear of negative repercussions. A topic that is both contemporary and of critical importance to law enforcement is high-speed pursuits. High-speed pursuits are incredibly dangerous. Not only are many people killed, agencies also lose millions in equipment and other resources. High-speed pursuits are receiving national attention, and agencies across the county are responding. If we were in an agency that was overly managed and relying on a risk avoidance model, what response might we expect?

As we have seen over and over, the risk avoidance approach is simple. High-speed pursuits result in enormous loss of life and property. Therefore, do not engage in high-speed pursuits. This is a classic risk avoidance approach.

If we choose to manage this risk instead, how might we respond better? We recognize that high-speed pursuits are dangerous. There is an inherent potential for loss or injury to the agency and the community it serves. Therefore, we develop a system to manage this risk better. The new system might include better training, new or modified policies, new communications plans, or new guidelines for when to initiate a pursuit. It might include the purchase of new equipment and technology. A risk manager will examine the problem and try to predict all of the potential outcomes. Having done that, the risk manager will seek solutions that will prevent the undesirable outcomes, while still allowing the preferred outcome—the apprehension and prosecution of the suspected violator. Risk management allows us to accomplish the desired mission, while preventing anticipated losses or injuries.

Risk management does not have to deal with life-and-death issues. During his presentation to the Law Enforcement Executive Development Seminar at the FBI Academy in January of 2004, Captain Graham related the following anecdote.

• • • • • • •

While working with the California Highway Patrol, he responded to a motor vehicle accident involving a truck belonging to a nationally recognized package carrier. While the accident was still being worked, a company risk management representative arrived on the scene. This company had thousands, if not tens of thousands, of trucks on the road every day. It recognized the risk and acknowledged that inevitably, accidents would happen. It further analyzed the risk and realized that the company would have to absorb loss to time and equipment. That was the limit of the acceptable risk, however. Other potential risks included insurance claims and lawsuits. The company had implemented a system to prevent those outcomes. This risk manager was empowered to make a monetary settlement with the other party on the spot. The risk manager assessed the damage to the other vehicle and made an offer. The other driver accepted it. The driver signed a waiver and release from seeking further compensation. The manager signed a check. Everyone left satisfied. Insurance claims, lawsuits, and negative feelings between the driver and the company were prevented. The California Highway Patrol and many other police agencies have adopted similar programs. This is risk management in action.

• • • • • • •

An in-depth lesson on risk management is outside the scope of this book. The concept is simply introduced here. The study of risk management could be a full-time vocation, and if you are interested, you should pursue more involved studies. However, the simple lesson is this: risk management can be applied to every aspect of law enforcement. If the outcome is predictable, then the outcome is preventable. Only by proactively examining an issue and working to predict the potentialities can we hope to prevent them. Unfortunately, most of the time, we choose to act without having undertaken this examination. When undesirable outcomes occur, we accept them as inevitable. This is certainly not the case. By embracing risk management, we work toward the betterment of our agency and the prevention of future loss.

• • • • • • •

While conducting training at the police academy, I had an opportunity to practice risk management as it applies to basic police training. In our academies, we have no control over the entry-level physical fitness of our candidate pool. The entry-level physical ability test is administered by another branch of government. Once a candidate passes that test, we are prohibited from administering any test that requires a higher level of fitness. Although we can give a fitness assessment, we can't eliminate anyone from training based on the results.

Several years ago, we received a new class at the academy. Upon their arrival, it was apparent that several of them were not in adequate physical shape to keep up with our training demands. Ordinarily, this is not a problem. Our academy sets a fairly rigorous pace right from the outset. Most student officers who are not in shape when they report quickly see the error of their ways and resign in the hope that they can improve their level of fitness and return in a future class. This class would prove to be a little different.

One of the student officers was extremely out of shape. During the initial physical fitness assessment, not only did he fail to complete the mile-and-a-half run in an acceptable time, he failed to complete it at all. We actually had to end that portion of the assessment before he finished walking it, because we ran out of time. This was going to be a challenge.

Once we ended the assessment, we attempted to engage this student in a conversation regarding his ability to continue training. He insisted that he was fine and would do well in training. When we expressed concern for his health and well-being if he continued to train, he put us off. He was from a police family, and he knew all he needed to know about coming to the academy.

Over the first several days of the academy, we became more and more concerned. This student officer did not satisfactorily complete any physical training events. Every session of calisthenics, running, strength training, or flexibility resulted in his being exhausted or injured. It wasn't getting any better, and we hadn't started any of the truly demanding combat-related training. During the second week of the academy, the physical training staff started integrating exercises to prepare the class for defensive tactics (DT). These exercises simulate DT moves and are designed to work the students' legs and core in the same way that blocks, kicks, and strikes do. The student in question did not show any improvement. We became more concerned. If he continued training, the outcome was easily predictable. He was going to get hurt.

We pulled him in for another meeting. We explained our concerns again. He wasn't hearing it. We had a staff member reach out to a member of his family to no avail. This was his dream, and there was no way that he was resigning. We took our concerns to the director. They were taken under advisement, but no action was taken. Eventually, I called my partner and lead DT instructor. I informed him of the situation. He reiterated to me that the DT program was fast-paced and had a limited number of classes. Based on the observations of this student, we agreed that if he were allowed to start the DT program, he would very likely suffer a serious injury. Again, the outcome was predictable. Was it preventable?

I sat down in the office and wrote a memo to the director. Basically, I outlined the position that as a staff instructor and defensive tactics instructor, it was my opinion that if this student was allowed to continue training, he would suffer a serious injury during defensive tactics. I went on to say that while the academy could allow him to continue training, the teaching staff were unwilling to accept responsibility for his health and well-being during the upcoming training. I also stated that allowing him to continue training was a predictable liability and that I was informing headquarters of my concerns. I put the signed original on the director's desk and faxed a copy to training headquarters. The student was gone within the week.

• • • • • •

CHAPTER 7

CONFLICT

Like *risk, conflict* is a word with an inherently negative connotation. Viewing it negatively, however, is problematic for any organization, especially a law enforcement agency. Simply put, conflict is a necessary force for change. Without it, we struggle to improve. The very concept of conflict, in and of itself, contains a conflict. As humans and as managers, we seek harmony. Unfortunately, harmony is not a naturally occurring state. The natural order for everything is a move toward chaos, or entropy. By continually seeking harmony, we fight the natural order. Snyder and Clontz point out the inherent dangers of this emphasis on harmony:

> Leaders' jobs are incredibly difficult because they must keep an eye on the future needs of their organizations and on the needs of the present. Too often, individuals wilt in the face of day-to-day crises and are timid and insecure about making hard choices. Many times the desire to avoid conflict and preserve harmony in the workplace is at the root of the problem. But preserving harmony may mean sacrificing the long-run interests of firms for short-term, imaginary gains. Leaders' efforts to appease and pacify discontented individuals and

groups, therefore, often reduce the ability of their firms to compete in the rapidly changing global market.[28]

So, if we must recognize and embrace conflict, what do we do?

Discussing conflict in regard to law enforcement brings about an interesting observation. As law enforcement practitioners, in essence, we thrive on conflict. The very nature of our work is to impose order on scenes of conflict. Whether it is responding to a domestic dispute, a civil disturbance, or an accident scene, police officers seek to instill order on otherwise chaotic situations. Without conflict, our jobs would be much simpler. Perhaps it is this aspect of law enforcement that causes us to extend this imposed order to our agencies and our larger lives.

Unfortunately, by doing this, we stifle our agencies and cause them to stagnate. In his presentations for the Drug Enforcement Administration, Dr. Harvey Goldstein teaches a block on conflict resolution. Dr. Goldstein comes to his conflict resolution expertise from a distinctly law enforcement point of view. Prior to becoming a noted lecturer on conflict and leadership, Dr. Goldstein served as a police psychologist and hostage negotiator. As discussed in the earlier passage on communication, Dr. Goldstein bases his conflict resolution strategy on empathic listening. Rather than seeking to avoid conflict, Dr. Goldstein advocates using empathic listening to manage and resolve it. Similar to the concept of managing risk, empathic listening allows us to manage conflict. By managing conflict, we put it to work for us rather than having it work against us.

Once we recognize that we can manage conflict and that, by managing it, we can produce progress, it becomes evident that conflict should not be feared and discouraged. Rather, it should be encouraged for specific purposes and managed. As law enforcement officers, we develop a certain amount of skill in resolving conflicts for those citizens we are sworn to protect. We utilize these skills to seek compromise and negotiate suitable outcomes. We do this at the most basic level as patrol officers responding to family disputes, and at a critical level in negotiating hostage situations. As police leaders, we should seek to utilize these same skills to manage and negotiate conflict within our agency, not with the goal of eliminating conflict but rather with the goal of seeking suitable outcomes for the organization. The reasons for doing this are many. One of the most important reasons is pointed out by Snyder and Clontz:

> Potentially, this obsession with harmony is more dangerous than any other problems leaders face; it threatens to drive out creative activity and the dedication and persistence of true change makers on whom we are so dependant for our future success. Leaders must guarantee that their firms encourage questioning, constructive dissension, and deep thinking. While some degree of harmony is necessary, excessive devotion to harmony can destroy an organization.[29]

Successful conflict resolution strategies place us in a position to harness conflict proactively and positively, and to bring about improvement. Again, Snyder and Clontz address the desirability of this type of approach:

> Because the world in which we live is changing so rapidly, firms must change constantly and improve continuously, if they hope to prosper and grow. Therefore, leaders must ensure that continuous improvement is a way of life for everyone in the organization. Since change, conflict and temporary disharmony are inextricably linked with continuous improvement, attempting to avoid them has the effect of thwarting progress.[30]

This notion brings us to our next critical element of leadership—embracing the value of change.

CHAPTER 8

CHANGE AND CREATIVE THINKING

> You can't lead anyone to where they are! Maintaining the status quo begs the efficiency of management. Only change benefits from aggressive leadership.
>
> —Sergeant Michael Wynn, DEA Leadership Fellow

> The human mind, once stretched to a new idea, never goes back to its original dimensions.
>
> —Oliver Wendell Holmes

Shortly after beginning my tenure at the DEA Academy, I had the opportunity to attend a class with Charles "Chic" Thompson. Chic, the author of the book *What a Great Idea!*, specializes in teaching and promoting creativity within organizations. His company, Creative Management Group, conducts training for numerous corporations and government agencies. As a creativity coach, Chic is committed to the notion of change. After attending his class, I was doing some leadership research and had the following epiphany. It occurred to me that many organizations, particularly government organizations, are seeking to foster and instill leadership among their supervisory personnel, but, at the same time, are seeking to maintain the status quo. These two simultaneous goals are, for all intents and purposes, mutually exclusive. The very concept of leading inherently involves movement.

If I am standing still and am perfectly content to remain standing still, I receive no benefit from dynamic leadership. Indeed, I will be better off with management. A manager will very efficiently enable me to remain where I am. However, if I want to move forward, to make improvements, and to advance my profession, I require leadership. Any leader who comes forward to assist me with this movement will, of necessity, encourage me to contemplate change.

Why is change necessary? If our organization or agency appears healthy and successful, why would we want to change it? If it's not broken, why fix it? These are profound questions. They are also questions that are frequently asked by managers who do not want to risk their little piece of power. Such managers ignore the realities of our world and of nature. No organization, no matter how healthy, can maintain the status quo indefinitely. If we are not active agents for our own changes, we simply force ourselves to be victims to unwanted change when it inevitably comes. We will be caught unprepared and will respond defensively. We dig in our heels, dig our trenches, and hope the forces of change will eventually pass. They seldom do.

In discussing this aversion to change, Snyder and Clontz make the following observation:

> Bureaucratic momentum and inertia in organizations can be overwhelming. They exert tremendous influence on the way people behave and cause them to spend their time and energy protecting the sta-

tus quo and pressuring others to conform to the conventional way of doing business.[31]

This adherence to institutional inertia can be devastating. Snyder and Clontz provide us with another anecdote to illustrate the destructive potential of inertia. Again, recognizing the obvious differences between business and government, it is not perfectly applicable. However, again, we recognize that government is destined to follow the path of business several decades later. Therefore, the story still has value as an example of how to think of situations.

> AT&T before its breakup in 1984 is another good example of this phenomenon at work. According to Charles Fombrun, "AT&T was an inertial system, lumbering into the future with an antiquated mission, a meaningless competitive strategy, and a complacent bureaucratic culture."
>
> This culture, and the bureaucracy that protected it, caused many of AT&T's problems. The company's employees failed to see beyond their day-to-day activities. Thus, they were unprepared for the rapid changes taking place that would forever change their company and the world in which we live.[32]

This example allows us to see that an organization, once regarded as one of the world's most successful, had allowed itself to become content with standing still. As a result, when the inevitable changes occurred, it was unprepared and unwilling to change to meet them. If this can happen to a giant like AT&T, it can certainly happen to our little agency. All law enforcement agencies have felt the effects of sweeping change. Equipment and technology are good examples: think of the change from revolvers to semiautomatic pistols to less-than-lethal weapons, from call boxes to radios to MDTs to wireless PDAs, and from typewriters and carbon paper to copy machines to word processors to document management solutions. Another example of external change can be seen in the continuous and ongoing effect of case law and new legislation on our enforcement activities. If we do not aggressively and proactively work to predict, embrace, and promote such changes, we will be forced to react to them as they occur.

If we acknowledge that change is an inevitable force and that, as leaders, we want to make change work for us rather than against us, how do we go about it? Chic Thompson would say that the answer lies in promoting creativity among our people. What exactly does this mean? As a young man, long before I had ever heard of Chic Thompson, I learned a valuable lesson. As a Boy Scout, I had been taught to leave every campsite better than I had found it. In a camping context, that meant picking up trash, even if I hadn't dropped it, and making small campsite improvements wherever I stayed. As an adult, I carried this philosophy into my professional life. As a young police officer, I made a conscious decision to find some way, every day, to improve my department. Whether through a new project, a new policy, a modification of a form, or a new system, I strove every day to create positive change. Ten years later, I received validation for this philosophy from Chic Thompson. "For truly great ideas will not flourish in organizations top-heavy with programs. Great ideas grow in organizations with a vision, a mind-set devoted to innovation and continuous improvement—to finding a better way every day."[33] Unfortunately for me, this was just my philosophy. My agency didn't exactly embrace it. Instead, it frequently attempted to thwart me. The organizational culture didn't exactly value creativity.

We've already discussed the value and necessity of vision. Chic alludes to it again in the above quote. How much more nimble and adaptable might our agencies be if we included the fostering of creativity in our vision statements? How much more effective might our vision be if, when we ask the question "Where do we want to be?" we considered all of the possibilities, not just the traditional ones? This idea is contrary to sound management practices. Encouraging creativity assumes risk and invites failure. However, true leaders recognize the value of risk and do not fear failure. Only when we step outside of the boundaries of our comfort zone and stretch our limits are true growth and change possible. Leadership coaches, including Stephen Covey, Alec Horniman, Harvey Goldstein, Carson Tucker, and many others, all teach this concept. It is at this boundary that creative thought and dramatic change are possible. We learn to spend more time in this boundary area by learning to increase our own creativity and the creativity of those with whom we work.

By embracing creativity and encouraging it in our organizations, we make much more possible. Without creativity, we find ourselves locked into a typical organizational mind-set, stymied by groupthink. This mind-set is also described by Chic:

> Many people use only a convergent method of idea making. They look at what is wrong with their situation, their environment, their company, their boss, their organization, their spouse. By focusing on the current state of affairs, they tend to limit their view of possibilities. By trying to come up with a solution, they often actively prevent solutions. By using only analytical and deductive reasoning, they force themselves down the rigid path of linear reasoning. The perils of this path were summed up by philosopher Emile Chartier: "Nothing is more dangerous than an idea when it is the only one you have."[34]

In teaching how to promote creativity, Chic delineates 20 Creative Rules and several other tenets. The 20 Rules are described in detail in his book *What a Great Idea!* Among the approaches he teaches, my favorite is, Ask the question, "What would I never do?" By using this approach to problem solving, you automatically encourage creative thinking. This question encourages out-of-the-box thinking. Instead of looking for the easy solution, my natural tendency, I should look for the approach that I would normally never take. This forces me to stop thinking with my rational, analytic brain and to engage my creative, intuitive brain. The answer may not be the solution I seek, but the process guarantees that I will utilize a different perspective. This enables creativity to flourish. According to Chic, "Creativity is the ability to look at the same thing as everyone else but to see something different."[35] By encouraging a number of people to take this approach, a variety of creative possibilities are encouraged.

Another one of Chic's concepts is, Avoid "Killer Phrases." Killer Phrases are typical, often automatic, responses to a creative idea. Chic describes a variety of Killer Phrases, but he also describes the process responsible for them:

> Psychologists have said that the human reaction to a new idea unfolds something like this, which we could call the Five Stages of Idea Acceptance:
>
>   1. It's irrelevant to this situation.
>
>   2. It's relevant, but it's unproven.
>
>   3. It's proven, but it's dangerous.
>
>   4. It's safe, but it's not sellable.
>
>   5. It'll sell; what a great idea![36]

Having discovered some of the value of creativity, the question is, How does creativity effect leadership? Let's rely on Chic to answer that question for us, too:

> In studying the qualities of good leaders, we have found that they routinely put on the shoes of people two levels above and below them.

For example, mid-level executives should look at a problem from the perspective of their boss's boss and their direct staff's employees. This broad perspective, gained through the Change-Your-Shoes approach to creativity, enables the executive to function and communicate as a leader, not just a manager. It encourages the creation of ideas that respond to the organization and its world as a system—and helps prevent ideas that only fix "my problem."[37]

A passion for proactive change and a commitment to encouraging the type of creativity that assumes that all things are possible are powerful tools for organizational leadership. By embracing change and creative approaches to change, we position our agencies to be proactive in determining their own futures. We do not have to be victims to unanticipated and unwanted change. As leaders, we can chart our agencies' course through turbulent times and make sure that, beyond remaining relevant, our agencies can serve as examples to our communities of what is possible.

• • • • • • •

Not long ago, I received a report from one of my unit supervisors. This sergeant wanted to draw my attention to the actions of one our patrol officers that had resulted in two arrests and the seizure of drugs, guns, and money. The sergeant had attached the arrest report and was requesting that the officer be commended.

I read through the materials and agreed with the sergeant that the officer's actions were indeed worthy of praise. Although it was not a major case, it was a solid patrol case. Essentially, the officer had developed information that the owner of a particular car did not have a valid license. After observing the vehicle, he had run the registration, confirmed that the owner's license was still not good, and had pulled the car over. On his approach, it was discovered that the driver was not the registered owner. He requested the driver's license and was informed that the driver did not have one. Based on this information, he continued with the traffic stop. The officer very quickly determined that there was more to this stop than an unlicensed driver. He called for some assistance. Members of the Drug Unit arrived. During the subsequent investigation, the officers discovered crack cocaine, money, and two guns. Both occupants were arrested.

Although the stop and the questioning were not picture-perfect, as we in law enforcement are aware, they seldom are. The facts of the matter are that none of the officers had done anything that was technically wrong and certainly nothing illegal. However, as is often the case, there were questions about the timing of the Miranda warnings and the nature of the detention. A debate broke out among our own personnel about whether the stop should have continued once the officer observed that the driver was not the registered owner. Based on these questions, it was obvious that the defendants would fight the stop and the arrests. There was certainly going to be a motion to suppress the evidence obtained from the stop. However, even if on some off chance we lost the case, we still had the drugs, money, and guns. Really, that was the bottom line.

As this discussion continued, one of my commanders argued that he didn't feel that we should offer a commendation to an officer who had taken actions that might not ultimately result in a conviction. I countered his argument with the fact that, conviction or not, the officer had interrupted what was obviously a distribution operation and removed two guns from the streets. He then countered with the fact that other officers had done similar things in the past and had not received any recognition. I acknowledged that argument but reminded him that in those cases, we weren't in command and hadn't had any control over the situation.

In my mind, the questions were simple. Did we want to take this opportunity to make a change in our organization's basic philosophies? As we moved forward as an agency, did we want to continue business as usual, or did we want to set a new tone? Did we want our officers to continue to believe that no matter what they did, their actions would be criticized in hindsight, or did we want them to feel that we were encouraging them to think independently, making proactive and aggressive decisions? The sergeant wasn't requesting a commendation for the entire case. Rather, he was requesting that the officer be recognized for going the extra mile and requesting additional expertise to take the stop to the next level. This debate clearly illustrated a division within our command staff, between traditional, conventional-wisdom thinking and proactive, outside-the-box thinking. This type of division is not unique to our agency. It is fairly commonplace in law enforcement agencies as we attempt to move our departments forward. However, it is exactly at the boundaries of divisions like these that change is possible.

• • • • • • •

CHAPTER 9

LEADING TROOPS

> Leadership is an analog skill in a digital world. You can't lead by email.
>
> —General John P. Jumper, former Chief of Staff, U.S. Air Force

Up to this point, our discussion has centered on leadership skills and concepts. However, none of this has any value if we can't put it into practice. As a new leader, we face two distinct leadership tasks. Both can benefit from our prior discussions. The first task, which we will address in this chapter, is obvious—leading those troops we are appointed to supervise. Having accepted the responsibility and privilege of leading, how do we go about it so that we can be most effective and best accomplish our mission?

The traditional view of leadership is leading down. The next part of our conversation is going to require us to re-examine this traditional view. Referring back to our conversation on loyalty, we discussed the possibility that as a supervisor, we serve as our troops' support staff. In essence, we work for them. Let's take this approach a little bit further.

In most organizations, and particularly in most paramilitary police agencies, the organizational model resembles a pyramid. The chief executive (chief, sheriff, director, etc.) is at the top. Below are the members of the command staff. The next level down may be bureau commanders, precinct commanders, or some other high-level supervisory officials. The levels continue downward, with more staff being added at each level. Eventually, we reach the first-level supervisors. Below them are the line troops, the producers who actually perform the job, produce the product, make the cases, or arrest the violators.

There is really nothing wrong with this model. It is time tested and very effective. The problem is one of perspective. By placing the chief and the managers at the top and the line officers at the bottom, we encourage hierarchical thinking that implies more importance with those personnel at the top and less importance at the bottom. What happens if we turn the model upside down (as in Chic Thompson's "What would I never do?"). This approach, advocated by the Blanchard Institute and other leadership coaches, changes our perspective.

At the very top of our model, we place the citizens we protect and serve. Below them are the line officers, our interface with the community. Since they are closest to the consumer, our line officers put forth our most important level of effort. Everything else the agency does or accomplishes must support their mission and their community interaction. Directly beneath the line officers are the sergeants or corporals. These first-level supervisors are responsible for providing support to the troops, channeling resources to them, providing training, and passing on direction from more senior supervisors. Below the sergeants are the lieutenants, shift commanders, or whatever other position supports the first-level supervisors. This level provides the same function for the sergeants that the sergeants provide to the line officers. Captains provide support and resources to the lieutenants. This continues down the chart to the most senior supervisor. The chief executive provides resources, training, direction, and support to his direct reports and to the entire agency. By turning the organizational model upside down, we encourage the perspective that leaders support their subordinates and not vice versa. Once we accept this premise, our responsibilities to and for our troops become readily apparent.

Having recognized that as supervisors we support our troops, what are our responsibilities? One of the most important was alluded to in our discussions on followership and fairness. As leaders, we must recognize that no matter how badly we may wish otherwise, our troops are not all the same. Every officer we work with is unique. They all have different experiences, abilities, goals, and desires. If we treat them all the same, we are being inherently unfair and run the risk of breeding hostility and contempt among them.

Consider the following example. As a sergeant, I have two direct reports working on the same squad. One is fairly experienced. She is competent and confident. She has demonstrated proficiency and is highly ambitious. The second officer is new. He is very inexperienced. His proficiency level is relatively low. He lacks confidence. While he is enthusiastic, he is currently content to be a patrol officer. If, as their supervisor, I elect to treat both officers the same way, I have to make a decision. For the sake of efficiency and effectiveness, I might decide to tailor my supervision to the younger officer. This would require close supervision and specific direction. I may provide constant training in relatively low-level tasks. While this approach may be appropriate for the junior officer, it is sure to breed resentment from the senior officer. That officer requires coaching and support. She wants to be encouraged in her ambition and given opportunities to expand her skills and advance her career. On the other hand, if I attempt to treat the junior officer as I should be treating the senior officer, then he will feel that I lack concern for him and that I am uninterested. He may feel lost and unwilling to perform any tasks he hasn't performed before. I am setting him up for failure.

The concept of adapting one's leadership style to the needs of one's followers is known as situational leadership. The term *situational leadership* was coined by Ken Blanchard and Paul Hersey. However the same concept is described by Kelley in his description of types of followers. Regardless of what name you give it or whose terms you use, the concept is the same: recognize the performance level of your troops and treat them as they deserve to be treated.

Once we have recognized that our troops require individual leadership styles, we must determine what specific leadership traits and functions we must perform to lead them effectively. The previous discussion of common leadership characteristics gives us a starting point. We must be supportive of them. We must provide them with the appropriate amount of direction. We must provide them with training and resources. We must advocate for them with our superiors. We must also insulate them from our superiors. We must be loyal to them and encourage loyalty among them. We must be ethical and demand that they act ethically also. We must be communicative with them; this requires that we relay the directives and expectations of the organization to them. We must also be communicative for them, relaying their wants, needs, and concerns to the rest of the organization. We must display courage both physically and organizationally. We must be willing to make the hard right decision for our people rather than the easy wrong one. We must set the example and lead by it. We must demonstrate our passion for our profession and excellence, and demand the same passion from them.

Having determined the specific leadership functions we will utilize with our troops, what is our overall goal? This is the simple part. Our goal is to enable our troops to perform the agency's mission in the most effective way possible.

As leaders, we do this by providing dynamic leadership to our troops. We rely on them to accomplish the mission. We trust them and prove ourselves deserving of their trust. We communicate the organization's vision to them and evaluate their success in relation to our vision. We empower them to carry out their tasks, secure in the knowledge that they have our support. We hold them accountable for the success of the mission, based on the fact that we have given them everything we possibly can to carry it out. We praise them frequently for their successes. When it is necessary to reprimand them, we accompany the reprimand with appropriate training to prevent the reprimanded be-havior in the future. We encourage them to provide the agency with their discretionary effort by providing them with opportunities to improve themselves and to advance.

How far can we go in providing dynamic leadership to our troops? How much freedom can we allow them to carry out the mission without micromanaging them? Some agencies have formalized this relationship of trust and enablement. In a presentation to the Law Enforcement Executive Development Seminar, Dr. John LeDoux provides an example of a formalized approach to employee empowerment. Dr. LeDoux displays a slide that describes the Phoenix [Arizona] Police Department's Employee Empowerment model. Each member of the Phoenix Police Department carries a card that asks the following questions:

- Is it the right thing for the community?
- Is it the right thing for the Phoenix PD?

- Is it ethical and legal?
- Is it something you are willing to be accountable for?
- Is it consistent with the PD's values and policies?

On the other side of the card is this statement:

> If the answer is YES to all these questions don't ask for permission ...JUST DO IT![38]

When I assumed command of a shift for the first time, I issued every one of my officers a similar card. I told each of them that I had faith in their abilities and in their desire to do the job. I told them that if they followed the above principles, I would protect them, even if they made a mistake and their action proved to be the wrong one. My officers appreciated the trust I placed in them and, for the most part, performed at an admirable level. More importantly, because they were willing to take action and be accountable for it, I had more time to deal with shiftwide issues and strategic matters. When I took command of the department, I provided all of my employees with the same model. The feedback that I received was universally positive.

When we adopt a similar leadership model, the entire agency will function at a higher level. Rather than the normally accepted management model that forces us to focus 80 percent of our efforts on 20 percent of our people, we get to spend an appropriate amount of time on each of our people. Mission accomplishment becomes our agency's lighthouse, fueled by the leadership we provide. Our mission becomes to provide the highest, most dynamic leadership we can, based on the principles we have learned.

CHAPTER 10

LEADING BOSSES

The second leadership task is not often thought about, and it is typically more difficult. Although it is widely recognized in business and industry, it is relatively uncommon in government, particularly in local government. This is the notion of providing leadership to our bosses. Typically referred to as "leading up," in our inverted model, we would actually be leading down. However, since this aspect is commonly referred to as "leading up," we will refer to it that way in our discussion. Leading up is leading the more senior levels of management in our organization. Providing leadership to our bosses is difficult, particularly if they are not receptive to being led by a junior level of management. The very concept begs this question: If we expect them to lead us, how can we also expect to lead them? The answer to that question begins with our earlier discussion of followership.

Once we have recognized the desirability of exemplary followers, we can seek to become one. And by becoming an exemplary follower, we ideally position ourselves to be able to lead our bosses. To review the earlier discussion, exemplary followers are actively involved in their agency's tasks. They are independent and engage in critical thought. They seize the initiative and are committed to the mission. At the highest levels, they are willing to stand up to their superiors. Carson Tucker, an adjunct professor with the University of Virginia's School of Continuing Education and Professional Studies, terms these followers the "loyal opposition." Loyal opposition works for the betterment of the entire organization, often by playing devil's advocate. They pose questions, provide analysis, and offer options.

Exemplary followers move the organization forward. One of the ways they accomplish this is by advancing their own careers, the careers of their direct reports, and the careers of their superiors. They are responsible for their own actions, their understanding of the job, and the actual performance of their tasks. They take ownership of their role and, therefore, are accountable.

Once you have established yourself as an exemplary follower, it is a short step to leading your bosses. The difficulty of serving in this capacity cannot be overestimated. However, the value cannot be ignored. Chic Thompson describes this conflict:

> Companies that truly encourage their people to buck the system are still in the minority. Leadership Expert Warren Bennis maintains that at least seven out of ten employees in American companies keep quiet when their opinions are at odds with their superiors'.
>
> Systems for rewarding those who dare to stand up and say "I've got a better way," are still news today. However, as more walls come down and competition keeps increasing, finding a better way will be in everyone's job description.[39]

This willingness to stand up and point out a better way is at the root of leading up. In any organization, it is impossible for one person to be an expert in every area of performance and production. In law enforcement agencies, the chief executive may have risen through the ranks or come in from another agency. He may have an expertise in any number of law enforcement skills, but the likelihood that he has expertise in every area of law enforcement is slim. Therefore, he relies on subject matter experts to provide information and knowledge about particular areas. As a leader, what is your area of knowledge? Is it accident reconstruction, training, use of force, or personnel? Are you providing your bosses with information about your area of expertise? As changes occur in a particular area, are you sharing that information with the organization? It is not enough just to train your troops. You may have to train your bosses also.

Another aspect of leading your bosses involves looking for opportunities to seize the initiative. If an agency is functional, the more narrow the span of control, the more responsibility a leader has for big-picture issues. While this is good for the health of the organization, it carries with it the danger that senior managers will miss some of the details. If senior managers are comfortable with their subordinates providing upward leadership, this allows an opportunity for first- and second-line supervisors to seek solutions to these "small" issues. On the other hand, the most proactive attempt to find a solution will be frustrated if the organization has not grasped the concept of leading up. If your boss has not entrusted and empowered you with the authority to seek solutions, you can't hope to find them. Earning this trust and authority is a critical part of leading your bosses. Once you have achieved this trust, you, as a leader, are poised to make invaluable contributions to your agency. Pursuing these contributions requires persistence and commitment.

> Uniquely rewarding opportunities present themselves rarely, whatever your business. When they do, you need to be both persistent in your pursuit of the opportunity and consistent in your efforts to make those above you understand its uniqueness. Even when your boss resists or fails to get it, the organization and cause you both serve deserves no less.[40]

Like every other aspect of leadership, leading bosses requires confidence. You must have the fortitude to stand up for what is right, even in the face of opposition and frustration. In the book *Leading Up: How to Lead Your Boss So You Both Win,* Michael Useem describes a number of historical episodes where leading up and failure to lead up had major impacts on the outcome. By examining these historic events, Useem puts upward leadership into an easily accessible perspective. According to Useem,

> Leadership has always required more than a downward touch: It needs to come from below as well as from the top, and leaders today must reach up as never before. As organizations decentralize authority, they put a premium on a manager's capacity to must support above as well as below. Command and control from on high are giving away to insight and initiative down under. Contemporary leaders aren't just bosses. They're self-starters who take charge, even when they have not been given charge.
>
> More upward leadership is essential. We have all known a supervisor or president, a coach or a minister, an officer or director who should have made a difference but did not. We privately complained, we may have even quit, but we rarely stepped forward to help them transcend their limitations and be the best boss they could be. Leading up is needed when a boss is micromanaging rather than macrothinking. Leading up is called for when a division president offers clear directives, but can't see the future, or when investors demand instant gain but need long-term growth.[41]

When an organization embraces a model of leading up, it is necessary to create some fundamental systems to foster the model. A culture of leading up does not just happen. It has to be built. Useem addresses this in his discussion of Marine Corps Lieutenant General Peter Pace:

A culture of upward leadership is built, not born. For that, a persistent insistence that all below you examine your proposals and challenge your errors is required. Asking those of lesser rank to say what they candidly think and complimenting them for doing so are small measures that can manufacture a big mind-set.[42]

Leading up is normally regarded as providing leadership to another level of organization. Useem points out that on occasion, leading up may require providing leadership at our own level of organization. This lateral component of upward leadership is critical to building support for initiatives we want to enact. Cultivating buy-in from our colleagues and associates is a vital first step before we take a new idea to our superiors.

Building lateral support for far-reaching change requires a top management team whose members can effectively back and execute the measure. The proper staffing of that team is your responsibility and not just that of the boss. The same is true of mobilizing the support of others whose backing and approval will be required for execution.[43]

Providing leadership to our bosses is an element that is often missing from contemporary organizations. Those organizations that have it are ultimately successful. Agencies that do not possess it risk failure. Today's work environment, complete with rapidly changing technology, personnel issues, increased liability, and all of the other potential risks, does not benefit from a traditional organizational model. Organizations must be flexible, embrace change, and value contributions from members at all levels. The recognition that every member of our agency may have something to contribute invites a culture of upward leadership. If, as leaders, we do not commit to fulfilling this role with the same passion we approach leading our troops, we are completing only half of the mission.

CHAPTER 11

LEADERSHIP CHALLENGES

Once we begin our leadership journey, we sincerely hope and expect to make some progress toward our desired goal. That is, we hope to become better, more effective leaders. Unfortunately, at some points along this path, there are naturally occurring pitfalls. Some of these stumbling blocks are commonplace and recurring. By discussing some of these, we can better prepare ourselves to deal with them. Identifying them ahead of time allows us to "when–then" visualize our response. Many law enforcement practitioners are familiar with this model of training. It allows us to approach a situation by thinking through a potential pitfall this way: When I encounter this situation, then I will respond this way. So what are some of these pitfalls?

GENERATIONAL ISSUES

During my year with the Drug Enforcement Administration in Quantico, the leadership challenge most often raised in all the classes and courses I attended was the integration of Generation X into the workforce. Nearly every time generational issues were raised, they were described as problems with Gen X. As a confirmed (and proud) member of Generation X, I took great exception to this characterization. In our discussions of this issue at Quantico, we eventually stopped looking at any one generation and, instead, began looking at generational issues in leadership. Generational issues are one of the greatest challenges facing the leader of today. The more generations that simultaneously coexist in the workforce, the more difficult the challenge becomes. Today, due to increased life expectancies and more years spent in the workforce, for the first time in history, we simultaneously have four sociological generations in the workforce. These generations—sometimes referred to as the civic generation, the baby boomers, generation X, and generation Y—all have different characteristics, different wants, and different needs. No one generation is any better suited to our mission. However, each of them is subject to misinterpretation and misunderstanding. If, as leaders, we don't strive to recognize the characteristics, limitations, and strengths of each generation, we cannot possibly capitalize on what they bring to the game.

This is not a discussion specific to generational leadership, and again, this subject is beyond the scope of this book. However, one anecdote from my Quantico experience may illustrate the importance of understanding generational leadership issues.

• • • • • • •

During one of the many development seminars I was allowed to attend, a chief executive from a large law enforcement agency opened a session with a complaint about Generation X. When asked to elaborate on the complaint, this chief stated Gen X employees are not loyal. They can't be counted on for the long haul. If they don't get what they want (quickly), they'll leave for another agency. They're not committed to the mission. They expect treatment to which they are not entitled (traditionally). Needless to say, as a member of the target of this diatribe, I was a little offended. In defense of my fellow Gen Xers, I offered this response:

> Members of Generation X (or any other generation) are as capable of loyalty and commitment as any older generation. However, their loyalty and commitment are not based on necessity or desperation. We will not offer our loyalty and commitment simply because we are grateful to have a job. Since we are generally more educated and more technically skilled than previous generations, we may have more options. Therefore, our loyalty comes at a cost. Leaders who want our loyalty and commitment must earn it by selling us on the organization's mission, history, vision, and goals. This interaction—the sales pitch—is a different kind of leadership for a different kind of employee. Once it has been accomplished, the Generation X employee may be as loyal as any other employee. However, her motivations for that loyalty are more than simple gratitude. Once earned, this employee's loyalty has the potential to be exponentially more productive than loyalty based on gratitude and desperation.

● ● ● ● ● ● ●

While conducting basic recruit training at the police academy, several other generational issues became apparent. During one of my first classes as a staff instructor at the police academy, I was involved in a situation that clearly painted for me some of the generational differences that existed in the workplace and the challenges that these differences were going to present for law enforcement. The specifics of the situation were rudimentary, but the issues that it raised have been repeated time and again throughout my career.

• • • • • • •

As the class got underway, the other staff instructors and I were conducting a routine uniform inspection. As is typical in an academy environment, the inspections served several purposes: they allowed us to teach raw recruits the proper way to wear and care for a police uniform, they provided a steady stream of minor disciplinary infractions to keep the students under stress, they allowed us to see how the students responded to criticism and adversity, and they gave us an opportunity to identify leaders within each class. Uniform inspections were not overly serious, but they also were not to be taken lightly.

As the inspection continued, minor uniform discrepancies were noted, and disciplinary violations were issued. A single uniform violation was nothing to be concerned about, but a combination of enough violations could lead to further disciplinary action. They could also be combined with disciplinary notices for other violations. After enough disciplinary violations of any type, a student officer could find herself fighting for her job. At one point, I became aware of a heated conversation between one of the other staff instructors and a student officer. I glanced over. The student officer was not from my agency, but he was from a smaller agency in my county. I always tried to take a particular interest in all of the student officers from home as a favor to my neighboring chiefs.

During the inspection, the staff instructor had observed this student officer's garrison belt. Although it technically met the description of "belt, black w/silver buckle," this belt was clearly not appropriate for uniform wear. It was thin and tooled. It obviously hadn't been purchased at a uniform store and didn't even appear to be leather. The staff instructor asked the student if that was the belt that his agency had provided him with. The student replied that it was. Finding this unbelievable, the staff instructor asked again if that was the belt that his department had issued to him. This would appear to be a simple question. If the belt was issued as part of his initial equipment, then the answer was yes. If the student had come by the belt in any other way, then the answer was no. It didn't seem too open to interpretation. The student again answered yes. To put the conversation to rest, the staff instructor told the student that we were going to call his chief and ask if the department had issued him this belt. The student started to qualify his earlier statements. Now we were all paying attention to this conversation.

Instead of taking the hit for the inappropriate belt, accepting the minor disciplinary notice, and getting a new belt, the student starting justifying his position. According to the student, the belt wasn't issued to him. However, it was "authorized." As his department did not have a lot of money, they had provided him with only a very basic uniform issue. His chief had then given him the equipment list and told him to purchase the remaining items. He had bought this belt as well as other small items and presented them to his chief for inspection. This opened up another line of questioning. We found it unlikely that any working police officer would have told this student that this particular belt was suitable to wear to the academy. Again, we told the student that we were going to call his chief and verify his statements about the item being "authorized." Again, he started to qualify his statements.

When I was at the Naval Academy, we referred to students who attempted to justify incorrect or inaccurate statements as "sea lawyers." In the Navy, a sea lawyer is a slimy creature who won't accept responsibility for his own mistakes and attempts to explain his way out of trouble. I have a particularly difficult time dealing with people whom I view as sea lawyers. They tend to irritate me.

I knew this student's chief. I also was very familiar with that agency and was aware that losing a student in training would have a detrimental effect on the department. I felt that I had an obligation to try to resolve the situation in a way that wouldn't end with the student getting dismissed from the academy. I started asking him very direct, close-ended questions that only allowed for yes or no answers. We had already caught him in one inaccuracy regarding whether the belt was issued. When confronted with that, he had stated that it was authorized. I wanted to make sure that he understood that while the uniform violation would get him written up, lying to us would get him kicked out. In response to my questions, he repeated his story that after he had purchased his remaining uniform items, his chief had inspected all of his equipment and approved it. Therefore, he insisted that it was authorized.

I left him with the other staff instructors and went into the office to call his chief. I got the chief on the phone and explained the reason for the call. The chief confirmed that the student had been given the equipment list and was instructed to purchase the remaining items on the list. I asked if there had been any specific instructions about where to buy equipment or the type of equipment. The chief stated that although there had been no specific instructions, it was understood that the equipment should be law enforcement-specific. I then asked the chief about inspecting the belt. The chief stated that there had been no equipment inspection. Once the student officer had been given the list, all of the equipment had been his responsibility.

This brought the situation to a whole new level. We brought the student officer into the office and started the whole line of questioning again. When confronted with the chief's explanation, the student started to qualify again. This time, he explained that the chief had "authorized" him to purchase the equipment on the list and that he had purchased items that he could afford. By the time the story had changed for the third time, we were out of patience. We dismissed the student officer and brought our concerns to the academy director. The director initiated an administrative investigation. By the time the investigation was concluded, the student had committed the inaccurate statements to a written report, and the academy was seeking to have him dismissed for untruthfulness.

As part of the administrative process, the chief appeared at the academy as part of a hearing with the director. During this hearing, the student insisted that he hadn't been untruthful, and the chief insisted that it was all a miscommunication and misunderstanding. The chief requested leniency and asked that the student be allowed to continue his training. Despite the staff's concerns and reservations about the student, he was allowed to continue his training and graduated with his class.

Shortly after this class graduated, I ran into this chief at a local law enforcement event. The chief related to me that as soon as the officer had joined the department full-time, he had engaged in a pattern of deceptive behavior toward the chief, culminating in his lying to the chief's face about seeking employment with another agency. The full extent of the deception wasn't realized until the officer resigned, without notice, leaving the department short-handed. The officer took a job with another nearby department. Final score: Staff Instructors–1, Bureaucrats–0.

• • • • • • •

This type of "circumstantial ethics" became more and more common in our dealings with younger police recruits. In a subsequent class, I was sitting in the staff office reading short written assignments. The topic was something innocuous, like department history or the meaning of the town's seal. As I read through them, I suddenly realized that I had read one essay already. I shuffled through the pile of essays that I had already completed, checking each one against the one on the desk blotter. I pulled out a second essay and laid it next to the first. Other than the name at the top of the page and the order of the paragraphs, they were identical—word for word. I took both essays and brought them to the director. After she read them, I went and pulled both student officers out of class.

I brought them into the office and confronted them with the discovery. These were both exemplary student officers. They were motivated and hardworking. They both had previous, part-time law enforcement experience. They both had college degrees. I couldn't understand why they would cheat. When I asked them, they denied any wrongdoing.

I placed the essays on the desk in front of them. They told me that since they lived together, they had worked on the assignment together, then printed out two copies. I pulled out a dictionary and showed them the definition of *plagiarism*. They told me that when they were in college, it was common for students to work on assignments together. When I asked them if they had been told to work on the assignment together, they responded that they hadn't been told not to. I was at a loss. I didn't even know how to respond to this. It wasn't that they wouldn't admit to any wrongdoing; they didn't even know that they had done anything wrong.

The above story shows a generational difference regarding ethics that became increasingly common. In other cases, we would find that younger student officers had no concept of "lying by omission." If they didn't specifically make a false statement to you, then it couldn't be a lie. They didn't understand that simply failing to make a statement or withholding information in response to an inquiry was also a lie.

As staff instructors, we were continually amazed at how often we would accuse a student of deception, only to have her insist that she had not deceived us. Over the course of several years, we had student officers take and distribute supplements and energy drinks while on duty, fail to report off-duty traffic crashes and law enforcement encounters, and withhold information that would bring discredit on the academy. In each and every situation, the student officers would tell us that because it wasn't specifically written in the academy rules and regulations or because we hadn't specifically asked, they didn't think that they were required to inform us. We were constantly frustrated.

Countless other areas may be affected by generational issues. The key to handling them is to recognize that those general characteristics that describe a generation are not inherently problems. They are instead characteristics that may be valuable to the organization. The challenge is to recognize them as such and capitalize on them. This is a mark of an effective leader.

FAILURE

Another of the major leadership challenges we face is coping with failure. All too often, fear of failure becomes a driving motivator in our behavior. This fear of failure can become so massive that it paralyzes us. Fear of failure can prevent us from taking chances, being creative, and seeking risk. Avoiding failure is no way to be a leader. Effective leaders make use of failure as a tool for improvement. It is only by trying and failing that we improve and grow. We do not learn by trying and succeeding. Instead, we accomplish most of learning as a result of failures—our own and others'.

When discussing the importance of failure, Chic Thompson offers this advice: "Fail fast." What Chic means is that it is not bad to fail—but if we let the failure linger, we invite problems. It is OK to take chances. It is OK for new ideas to fail. However, the longer we take to realize this idea is a failure, the more time, resources, and effort we have wasted on it. Therefore, while we want our new ideas to succeed, if they do fail, we want them to fail quickly.

Once we recognize that failure is OK and that fast failure is preferable to slow failure, we can learn to manage failure. For example, when creating a new idea or program, we can build in a check valve to allow for fast failure. Often, however, we do not do this.

• • • • • • •

At one point in my career, I was tasked with revamping our in-house training program. I welcomed the opportunity and challenge. I thought our training program was out-of-date and inadequate. The new training program would be my legacy. I built it from the ground up. I got buy-in from the troops, the unions, and the administration. I selected the curriculum and documented the lesson plans. After all this, I put together a training schedule for the first year. Let me repeat that—I scheduled training for a year. When I sold it to the bosses and got authorization to implement it, it was a year-long plan. This was an untested and novel program. I had no reason, other than my own arrogance, to believe it would succeed.

When the program was implemented, it became obvious within the first several weeks that I had not anticipated some fairly sizeable problems. However, because I had not allowed for fast failure and had not built in a check valve, I had no way of stopping the monster I had created. My superiors expected a year's worth of training. When I reported on my issues and concerns, the unspoken message I received was to press on and make it work. I had not allowed an escape route. In hindsight, what I should have done was develop the plan for one rotation. At the end of that rotation, I should have scheduled a meeting for all of the principles to address and repair all of the issues that had been raised. If they could not be repaired, the program should have been scrapped. This would have been a fast failure check valve.

• • • • • • •

LEADER–FOLLOWER RELATIONSHIPS

Another leadership challenge that was frequently mentioned in the development seminars I attended was "first-level supervisors." This was a catch-all phrase chiefs and sheriffs used to describe subordinates with whom they were unhappy. After asking some difficult questions, most of the bosses dealing with this issue would admit that the problem was not specifically first-level supervisors (e.g., corporals and sergeants). Rather, it was a problem created by supervisors supervising the same unit, shift, squad, or team that they had just served on. Regardless of the level of command, if a supervisor was responsible for directly supervising those people with whom he had recently been peers, difficulties often arose. The closer the supervisor was to the line level (first-level supervisors), the more severe and pronounced the problem. As leaders, our challenge is to recognize these potential difficulties and have a plan for dealing with them.

In most police agencies, particularly most small agencies, newly promoted supervisors are of necessity going to supervise their colleagues and peers. This is a particular challenge for the newly promoted supervisor. Yesterday, these peers were my friends and partners. I relied on them for support and backup. I trusted them with my well-being and my life. Today, I am their boss. I know these people. I naturally want to maintain my relationship with them. Unfortunately, I am no longer their peer. I am their supervisor. I am responsible for their performance, training, discipline, development, etc. My relationship with them cannot be the same. If I try to maintain it, I will fail as a leader. When I fail as a leader, I fail my organization, my mission, and my troops. I am not doing anyone any favors when I choose not to do my job.

SUCCESSION PLANNING

Another leadership challenge facing today's leaders is the concept of succession planning. Business and industry are leaps and bounds beyond government in this area. However, if we don't consider it, we fail the future of our agency. *Succession planning* is a fancy way of saying "planning for the future." This is a very difficult task for many leaders, particularly police leaders. Succession planning requires that we as leaders identify those subordinates who have the potential to serve in our capacity. Having identified them, we provide them with the training, development, and opportunities to fulfill that potential.

To many people, this appears to resemble career suicide. The typical government attitude is to prevent others from gaining the ability to replace us. If I protect my knowledge, skills, and abilities, I become indispensable. The agency will need me. However, this is a narrow-minded and backward-thinking approach.

Succession planning takes another approach. By utilizing succession planning, we develop our future replacements. By developing them, we ensure the future of our organization, our mission, and our vision. By developing talented subordinates, we secure their loyalty and their discretionary effort. They will give us their best and follow us diligently. We do not risk them ever replacing us, until we choose to or need to leave. When they do replace us, we leave a legacy of qualified, skilled, and determined followers who will step into leadership roles prepared and with the desire to lead.

CHAPTER 12

WHERE DOES MANAGEMENT FIT IN?

Up to this point, I have taken a relatively negative stance on the science of management. I chose to do this more to make a point than to disparage all management practices. Needless to say, in today's complex organizations, sound management practices are an absolute necessity. However, if we refer to Chapter 1, "Management Versus Leadership," it is easy to see that sound management must follow effective leadership for the organization to be fully successful. Let us examine how management can assist us to be better leaders.

A wide range of management models is available today. However, since we started this journey with the POSDCORB model, let us continue with it. As a reminder, POSDCORB stands for Planning, Organizing, Staffing, Directing, Coordinating, Reporting, and Budgeting. No modern organization can survive without some version of these areas. If addressing these issues is the overall concern of an organization's supposed leaders, we are stuck in a management paradigm. If, on the other hand, these concerns become tools to enable us to lead our troops better, we are utilizing management to further our leadership mission.

Law enforcement agencies are well acquainted with planning concerns. In today's day and age, we try to have a plan for everything. If we become slaves to our plans and planning, we are definitely managing. On the other hand, plans can allow us to free up a significant amount of time to exercise leadership tasks. Let's take a look at one particular type of plan with which most law enforcement personnel are familiar.

Whether they refer to it as "Policies and Procedures," "Standard Operation Procedures," the "Manual," or some other name, most agencies have a set of written plans and orders which covers situations that occur regularly. Well-constructed policy manuals are comprehensive, meaning that they cover a wide variety of circumstances. However, they are also general enough that they don't restrict discretion and independent thought. Policies should be regarded as a helpful set of guidelines rather than the disciplinary tools they are often considered. Looking at the manual as a helpful tool is easy. Can you imagine an organization with no policies? Leaders would have to make a new decision for every situation that arose, even if the situation had been seen before. When we have policies in place, we don't have to make the same decision over and over. Policies are meant to give leaders more flexibility. Instead, they often become the cage in which leaders trap themselves.

Organizing is another management concern that, once completed, allows a leader more time and freedom. By structuring the agency in a particular way and making the structure widely known and recognizable, leaders know where to focus their efforts. Organizing allows us to know which subordinates are our responsibilities and which are not. It also tells us where we can go for assistance or support. Organizing must consider a wide range of variables. It considers our people, but it must also consider resources, funding, politics, and other issues. Most of these are outside of the realm of leadership. For leaders to have the time and flexibility to work with and for their troops, these issues need to be decided elsewhere. The same leader may be leading troops and designing an organization, but the troops should not have to be aware of the leader's organizing responsibilities.

Staffing is another component of organizing. It allows an agency to determine where the agency's resources are best allocated. This is an agencywide concern. Although the needs of the troops may be (and often should be) considered, staffing addresses the needs of the agency first. Effective staffing allows the agency to function at maximum efficiency. Although it is essential to sound operations, staffing is also not a leadership concern.

Directing may be viewed as both a management and a leadership concern. However, as it is typically regarded in the POSDCORB model, directing refers to agencywide directives. The development of agencywide directives is a management concern, while the delivery of these directives is a function of leadership. Directives are developed with the intent of better allowing the agency to accomplish its goals. This is about efficiency. Communicating the agency's directives to the troops normally benefits from sound leadership. This is where efficiency can be married with increased effectiveness. Leaders allow the organization to gain buy-in for the directives from the line troops.

Coordinating is another management concern that may benefit from a leadership touch. Overall coordination among the organization's divisions or bureaus is a management issue. Managers must serve as a conduit among the agency's various missions and concerns.

However, leaders must provide coordination also, coordinating the efforts of their own troops. This is particularly pertinent at the line levels of an organization and in field operations.

Reporting is also a management issue. At a general level, sound reporting practices benefit the agency or organization as a whole. Reports allow the agency to document its operations and efforts. Although individual members of an organization may sometimes benefit from sound reporting practices, generally reports are required for the benefit of the organization.

Budgeting is another management concern. Although no agency can survive without sound budgetary practices, the day-to-day financial concerns are outside of the realm of leadership. Leaders must direct their energies at allowing their people to complete the mission regardless of budgetary restraints on resources. Leaders do their best with what they have. Managers provide the leaders with the resources they need to fulfill their mission. No leader can afford to concern himself with budget concerns when his people need him to lead the way.

I want to repeat that I do not want to give the impression that management is unnecessary. Management is very necessary. Any complex organization must be managed. The concerns of planning, documenting, funding, and reporting are very real and must be addressed. However, these are concerns for the entire organization. The organization is composed of individual people, and these individuals beg to be led. Systems can be managed, but workers must be led. This realization leads Covey to conclude that management must follow leadership.

Having explored the role that management plays in the leadership question, how do we accomplish management? Many law enforcement agencies address management by creating staff positions. These positions, outside of the operational chain of command, handle the overall management concerns of the organization. They provide the policies, structure, orders, and budget to the line troops. Within the confines of these parameters, field leaders guide their troops to accomplish the goals and mission of the agency. Since the two areas are so different, they must be kept separate. This is often difficult in small agencies. Out of necessity, some leaders will be tasked with management functions, which are often collateral duties. These duties may become such a burden that the leader is tempted to stray from leadership responsibilities to accomplish management responsibilities. Leaders must remember that their first responsibilities are simultaneously to the mission and to the people. Everything else is secondary.

On the other hand, every leader benefits from a better understanding of staff/management functions. If you know what management is trying to accomplish and why it is doing certain things, you will be better prepared to explain to and advocate for your people. For this reason, exposure to staff functions is an excellent way for leaders to expand their big-picture view of the agency. If given a chance to serve in a staff capacity, consider it a career-expanding move. Be willing to look at things from another perspective. Broader knowledge of your organization can only improve you as a leader.

CHAPTER 13

OUR PERSONAL LEADERSHIP COMMITMENT

We started this journey together by looking at the dichotomy between the management and leadership paradigms. An examination of the shortfalls created by valuing management over leadership led us to a look at what leadership can be and what it can do for us. I hope I've managed to convince you that any organization will benefit from an increased commitment to leadership. If I have and you've committed to increasing your leadership potential, as I have, how do you go about it? There is no one recipe for success in becoming a leader, but I'd like to share a few things that I have found beneficial in my personal journey.

To begin with, you must commit to constant and ongoing improvement as a leader. Every day that you choose to continue the responsibility and privilege of leading other people is another day to improve. When you are no longer willing to improve your personal leadership, you are no longer worthy of your people's trust and respect. Constant improvement need not be difficult.

One of the most valuable tools I've found to improve my personal leadership is reading. There are so many books out there on leadership and leading that reading all of them is a virtual impossibility. It also isn't necessary. What is necessary is to expose yourself to different ideas. Pick a leadership book and read it. Don't read it with the goal of discovering a completely new way of doing things. Read it critically. Go into each book with the "good bag/bad bag" theory in mind. Examine it for ideas and techniques you can buy into. Dissect it to find things that you disagree with or don't believe you can incorporate into your personal style. When you find something that you don't feel comfortable with, move past your knee-jerk reaction. Re-examine it with a more critical eye and give it another chance. Only after you've turned it over a couple of times should you throw it into your "bad bag."

Don't limit yourself to books that seek to teach leadership. Select a biography of a famous leader. Dive into the history of a significant event with leadership challenges. Read with the goal of discovering what made other leaders great, and borrow from the great ones. Military leaders, politicians, diplomats, corporate heads, and other important figures have lessons to offer. Take advantage of them.

Once you've read a book, don't keep the lessons to yourself. Discuss it with friends, colleagues, and other leaders. Recommend it to your peers and colleagues. Better yet, give it to them and ask them to read it. Provide some measure of leadership to your peers in their leadership journey. Share the wealth.

Don't stop with one book. Set a goal for yourself. Make a commitment to read one leadership-related book a month, one a quarter, or two a year. Stay involved in your leadership studies. Make an attempt to stay current with what is out there.

If reading isn't your thing or if it doesn't seem to be enough, take a leadership class. Most law enforcement personnel and other professionals are interested in receiving advanced training. Unfortunately, most of us would prefer to pursue training in our areas of specialization. What we must realize is that leadership is our most important specialty. We should pursue leadership training with the same energy and vigor that we pursue other training.

Leadership classes are readily available. Most federal law enforcement agencies offer training that is available to other agencies. Nearly all of the widely known professional organizations offer clinics and schools that focus on leadership issues. Also, many private organizations offer courses that range from one day to several weeks. If none of these is available to you, look to your local colleges or businesses. Ask them if you can audit a class or join their executives for the training they offer.

Taking classes in leadership allows you not only the chance to seek additional education, but also an amazing opportunity to network. In the leadership development courses that I've been privileged to attend, I have easily learned as much from my classmates as from the instructors. Surrounding yourself with other successful leaders will reinforce your commitment to leadership, expand the number of people to whom you can look to for assistance and support, and allow you to increase the number of tools in your leadership "good bag."

The next thing that you can do to commit to the improvement of your personal leadership mission is to practice. Seek and create opportunities to provide leadership. Do it in your organization by volunteering for or creating units and programs that require leadership. Do it outside of your organization by joining community groups, civic organizations, or youth organizations that will allow you to serve in a leadership role. Remind yourself that leaders must choose to lead. Choose to lead wherever and whenever you can.

Once you have committed to improving your personal leadership mission, it may be beneficial to formalize it. In classes and conversations, Colonel Danny McKnight has repeatedly emphasized the importance of a written leadership philosophy. A leadership philosophy is a document that allows you to summarize your personal commitment to leadership. It allows you consider what leadership means to you and what your people can expect of you. Once you have written it, you can share it with your troops. This sets the stage for your future interactions with them.

When I decided to take Colonel McKnight's advice and write my personal leadership philosophy, I also decided to make it a living document. Since my career does not require constant command changes, it is not necessary for me to write a new philosophy for every move. However, as I grow and change as a leader, my philosophy must change. Therefore, a living philosophy requires that it be revisited frequently. Each step I take or change I make requires that I adjust my philosophy and edit the document. In this way, my philosophy constantly reflects my beliefs and my commitment to leadership.

The written leadership philosophy not only serves as notice to subordinates as to what they can expect; it also serves as a reminder for each of us as leaders. Each time I sit down to edit it, I also reread it. By frequently reading my version of my philosophy, when I slip and fail to live up to my commitment, I readily understand how I need to improve. A written leadership philosophy serves as the chart that allows me to remain on course during this journey.

Leadership Philosophy of Michael James Wynn

As a law enforcement supervisor, I recognize the need for me to demonstrate and provide true leadership to my subordinates, my peers, and my agency. To this end, I will strive to hone and improve my leadership abilities. As a leader, I will attempt to be ...

Mission-oriented: I recognize that the mission of law enforcement is not just to enforce the law and secure the lives and property of citizens. I recognize that our duty is to improve the quality of life of our residents. I am committed to identifying and attempting any reasonable tool that can be used to this end. All aspects of the law enforcement mission are equally important, and all aspects will be given due attention.

Safety-driven: The only consideration more important than the accomplishment of our mission is the safety of our people. To that end, I will make every effort to ensure that my people have the best technology, equipment, training, and information to guarantee their safety and security. No member of any unit under my command is expendable, and no officer should ever be injured or killed because of circumstances that could have been foreseen and prevented. Officer health and safety is my primary concern.

Passionate: According to Lieutenant Colonel David Grossman, police officers are the "sheepdogs" that stand the line between the citizen sheep and the perpetrator wolves. As a sheepdog, I recognize that my role in life is to stand ready to protect those I have sworn to serve. There can be no higher calling. This is my duty. This is my passion. Should there ever come a day that I am not passionate about my chosen profession, I have stayed too long.

Approachable: As a law enforcement officer and a law enforcement leader, I recognize that most people have difficulty approaching the police, and most officers have difficulty in approaching their bosses. Nothing is gained by anyone when we build walls between us. As a professional law enforcement executive, I will be approachable to my constituents and to my subordinates. I will engage in empathic listening and communicate to people that I value their contributions. More importantly, I will serve as a mentor and guide to my troops. I will never mistake knowledge for power and will never withhold information from my troops to protect my own position. I have made it this far with the help of many people and will provide the same help to my people at every opportunity.

Trustworthy: As a police officer, I have sworn to a sacred trust. I will be worthy of that trust. I will show myself to be honorable, ethical, and forthright.

Trusting: As a police leader, I am duty-bound to develop my subordinates' abilities. I can accomplish this only by placing my trust in them. I must trust them to do the right thing when called upon and give them the freedom to fail. No one is served by my managing every aspect of their performance.

Competent and confident: As a professional law enforcement officer, I will work constantly to improve and increase my technical skills. I will seek any training that I can to become a better performer. I will use my improved skills to promote my self-confidence. I am trained to handle any situation that I may encounter. I will survive any encounter that I engage in.

Training-focused: As a police leader, I recognize that the only way that knowledge is increased and skills improved is through constant training. I will provide constantly for the training of my troops. Any topic or subject that may improve the performance of my agency is a potential training topic. I will encourage every one of my people to become an instructor or recognized expert in his field of interest.

Professional credentials support a professional organization. As a law enforcement trainer and instructor, I will communicate my passion to my students and troops. I will constantly improve those I work with by training them to a higher level of performance.

Compassionate and caring: I will never forget that before I am a police officer, I am a human being. I will remember that all people deserve basic compassion and respect. Within those limits required by officer safety concerns, I will treat all people with concern, compassion, and caring. I will always remember that I am a servant of the people and approach my contacts with them from the perspective of providing a service. I will be cognizant of their needs and wants.

Visionary: As a law enforcement professional, I recognize that law enforcement is a dynamic and rapidly advancing profession. Since nothing remains constant for long, I will focus on the future rather than on the past and present. I will develop my vision for myself, my agency, and my community. I will communicate that vision to all of my subordinates and constituents. I will share my vision with my fellow community leaders and my superiors to keep them informed. I will be an advocate for the forward progress of my people, my agency, and my community.

Creative: I recognize the value of thinking outside the box. As a law enforcement professional, I will strive to find the creative answer or "new" solution to old problems. I recognize that the very idea of leadership implies some movement toward a goal. I will not allow myself, my troops, or my agency to stagnate in the status quo. As a law enforcement problem solver, I believe that any problem is solvable and one of us has the answer.

Providing leadership to other people is perhaps the most unbelievable responsibility any person can have. It is also the most amazing privilege we can be allowed. When we decide to become leaders, we are entrusted with the hopes, dreams, and well-being of those we lead. Treating leadership as an appointed position and approaching it with only the tools currently at our disposable is a disservice to our people, our organization, and ourselves. Leadership is an ever-changing and ever-expanding journey. By deciding to embark on that journey, we place ourselves in a position that is rife with pitfalls and obstacles. The only way that we can hope to avoid some of those obstacles is by continuing to learn and improve as a leader. A commitment to leadership is a commitment to constant improvement—improvement of our people, our organizations, and, of course, ourselves.

BIBLIOGRAPHY

Bracey, Hyler, Jack Rosenblum, Aubrey Sanford, and Roy Trueblood. *Managing From the Heart.* New York: Dell Publishing, 1990.

Covey, Stephen R. *The 7 Habits of Highly Effective People: Powerful Lessons in Personal Change.* New York: Simon and Schuster, 1989.

Duhon, Barbara, ed. *International Association of Chiefs of Police: Leadership in Police Organizations.* New York: McGraw Hill Custom Publishing, 2002.

Gilmartin, Kevin, M. *Emotional Survival for Law Enforcement: A Guide for Officers and Their Families.* Tucson, AZ: ES Press, 2002.

Giuliani, Rudolph, W. *Leadership.* With Ken Kurson. New York: Miramax Books, 2002.

Hughes, Richard L., Robert C. Ginnett, and Gordon C. Curphy. *International Association of Chiefs of Police (IACP) Leadership in Police Organizations.* New York: McGraw Hill

Kelley, Robert E. *The Power of Followership.* New York: Doubleday, 1992.

LeDoux, John, C. *Executive Leadership.* Training program for the Federal Bureau of Investigation, 2004.

Maxwell, Ronald F. *Gettysburg.* Directed by Ronald F. Maxwell. Atlanta, GA: Turner Entertainment, 1993.

McKnight, Danny. *Commitment to Leadership.* Presented at the DEA Training Academy, April 15, 2004.

Merriam-Webster. *Merriam-Webster's Collegiate Dictionary.* 11th ed. Springfield, MA: Merriam-Webster, 2003.

Powell, Colin. "A Leadership Primer." As written by Oren Harari. HR Chally Group. www.chally.com/enews/powell.html.

Snyder, Neil H. and Angela P. Clontz. *The Will to Lead: Managing with Courage and Conviction in the Age of Uncertainty.* Chicago: Irwin Professional Publishing, 1997.

Thompson, Charles. *What a Great Idea!* New York: Harper Collins, 1992.

Useem, Michael. *The Leadership Moment.* New York: Three Rivers Press, 1998.

———. *Leading Up: How to Lead Your Boss So You Both Win.* New York: Three Rivers Press, 2001.

NOTES

1. McKnight, Danny, *Commitment to Leadership,* presented at the DEA Training Academy, April 15, 2004.

2. Powell, Colin, "A Leadership Primer," as written by Oren Harari, HR Chally Group, www.chally.com/enews/powell.html (accessed March 31, 2008), Lesson 18.

3. Covey, Stephen, R., *The 7 Habits of Highly Effective People: Powerful Lessons in Personal Change* (New York: Simon and Schuster, 1989), 102.

4. Ibid., 101.

5. Ibid.

6. Ibid.

7. Snyder, Neil H. and Angela P. Clontz, *The Will to Lead: Managing with Courage and Conviction in the Age of Uncertainty* (Chicago: Irwin Professional, 1997), iii.

8. Merriam-Webster. *Merriam-Webster's Collegiate Dictionary,* 11th ed. (Springfield, MA: Merriam-Webster, 2003).

9. Maxwell, Ronald F., *Gettysburg,* directed by Ronald F. Maxwell (Atlanta, GA: Turner Entertainment, 1993).

10. Hughes, Richard L., Robert C. Ginnett, and Gordon C. Curphy, *International Association of Chiefs of Police* (IACP) *Leadership in Police Organizations* (New York: McGraw Hill), 152.

11. Bracey, Hyler, Jack Rosenblum, Aubrey Sanford, and Roy Trueblood, *Managing From the Heart* (New York: Dell Publishing, 1990), 47–48.

12. Ibid., 110.

13. Covey, *7 Habits,* 196.

14. Ibid., 235.

15. Bracey et al., *Managing From the Heart,* 50.

16. Thompson, Charles, *What a Great Idea!* (New York: Harper Collins, 1992), 18.

17. Giuliani, Rudolph, W., *Leadership,* with Ken Kurson (New York: Miramax Books, 2002), 34.

18. Ibid., 34–35.

19. McKnight, *Commitment to Leadership.*

20. Ibid.

21. Ibid.

22. Merriam-Webster, *Dictionary.*

23. DEA Organizational Leadership Dynamics. 2002.

24. Covey. p. 55.

25. Covey. p. 143.

26. Getty, Jim, DEA Academy, April 14, 2004.

27. Merriam-Webster, *Dictionary.*

28. Snyder and Clontz, *The Will to Lead,* 59.

29. Ibid., 60.

30. Ibid.

31. Ibid., 62.

32. Ibid., 61.

33. Thompson, *What a Great Idea!*

34. Ibid., 11.

35. Ibid., 4.

36. Ibid., 24.

37. Ibid., 108.

38. LeDoux, John, C., *Executive Leadership* (Training program for the Federal Bureau of Investigation, 2004), 7–8.

39. Thompson, *What a Great Idea!,* 33.

40. Useem, Michael, *Leading Up: How to Lead Your Boss So You Both Win* (New York: Three Rivers Press, 2001). 229.

41. Ibid., 1.

42. Ibid., 174.

43. Ibid., 241.

ACKNOWLEDGEMENTS

This book is dedicated to all of the police officers with and for whom I have had the pleasure of working during my career and to the men and women of the Drug Enforcement Administration's Leadership Development Unit, who helped me gain some of the tools to do that work better.

Most importantly, this book is dedicated to my mother, Frances, who taught me that anything is possible, and to my devoted wife, Vicki, who stands beside me as I try to prove it.

UNDERSTANDING AND MANAGING GENERATIONAL DIVERSITY

The dilemma:

- Increasingly diverse workplace

- Employee differences can be both a source of frustration and energy

- In the field of law enforcement, differences based on age and experience can be difficult to manage

- What are the general characteristics of our employees that may be based on their age and experiences?

- How do we learn to recognize and deal with these characteristics?

- What are some strategies that we can employee to make these differences work for our organization?⊠

We have reached a unique point in history:

- Four generations in the workforce at the same time

- People are working longer

- People have a different view of retirement

- People are living longer

- As a result, many people will be retired for as long (or longer) than they worked

In the workplace, many organizations are much "flatter."

- Decentralization

- Pushing authority to lower levels

- "Community Policing"

The result is more contact between an increasingly diverse workforce. The presence of different generations in the workplace can cause several leadership challenges:

- Fear

- Frustration

- Resentment

- Disdain

- Retention

A leader's goal is to recognize generational differences, including:

- What eras define different generations

- What experiences defines them

- What are the characteristics of each generation?

DEFINING GENERATIONS: TRADITIONALISTS

- AKA Builders, GI Generation, Hero Generation, the Greatest Generation

- Born approximately 1922–1945

- Ages 62–85

- Not many remaining in our sworn workforce, but there are a few holdouts.

Shared Formative Experiences:

- WWI and WWII

- Great Depression

- Atomic Bomb

- Rationing

DEFINING GENERATIONS: BABY BOOMERS

- Born approximately 1943–1964

- Ages 43–64

Shared Formative Experiences

- Cold War

- Civil Rights

- Space Race

- Political Assassinations

- Vietnam

- Watergate

- Energy Crisis

DEFINING GENERATIONS: GENERATION X

- AKA Baby-buster, Busters

- Born approximately 1961–1983

- Ages 24–46

Shared Formative Experiences

- Roe v. Wade

- Challenger explosion

- Fall of the Berlin Wall and Soviet Union

- AIDS

- First Gulf War

- Clinton Administration

DEFINING GENERATIONS: MILLENNIALS

- AKA Generation Y, Bridgers, Mosaics, Net Generation

- Born approximately 1978–2000

- Ages 7–29

Shared Formative Experiences

- Oklahoma City bombing

- Internet

- September 11, 2001

- School shootings

- Economic Globalization

RECOGNIZING GENERATIONAL CHARACTERISTICS

Major Influences

- Traditionalists: Family and Church

- Boomers: Family and education

- Generation X: The media

- Generation Y: Friends, media, celebrities

Family

- Traditionalists: Close family (nuclear family)

- Boomers: Dispersed family (increased divorce rates)

- Generation X: Latch-key kids

- Generation Y: Dual families, non-traditional families

Education

- Traditionalists: Education is a dream

- Boomers: Education is a right

- Generation X: Education is a tool to get there

- Generation Y: Education is an incredible expense

Marriage

- Traditionalists: Married once

- Boomers: Married/Divorced/Re-married

- Generation X: Single parents/blended families

- Generation Y: To Be Determined

War

- Traditionalists
  - Win the war
  - War is a common cause of civilized nations

- Boomers
  - Why war?
  - War is a creation of the military-industrial complex

- Generation X
  - Watch a war
  - 100 hour ground conflict
  - Casualties measured in hundreds

- Generation Y
  - War on Terror
  - Indefinite timetable
  - Constant casualty counts

Attitude Toward Authority

- Traditionalists
  - Authority endures
  - Honor and respect authority

- Boomers
  - Replace authority
  - Challenge leaders
  - Never trust anyone over 30

- Generation X
  - Ignore leaders
  - Work in spite of them

- Generation Y
  - Leaders must respect you
  - Choose your own boss

Work

- Traditionalists: Work is an inevitable obligation

- Boomers: Work is an exciting adventure

- Generational X: Work is a difficult challenge

- Generation Y: Work is a means to an end

Career

- Traditionalists
    - Committed company worker
    - One company for life
    - Live to work

- Boomers
    - Disgruntled company worker
    - Downsizing
    - Lay offs

- Generation X
    - Suspicious worker
    - Organization doesn't value the individual
    - Don't depend on any one company
    - Knowledge workers can transfer KSAs

- Generation Y
    - Entrepreneurial
    - Work for yourself

- Work to live

PERSONAL CHARACTERISTICS

- Traditionalists
  - Hard workers
  - Savers
  - Patriotic
  - Loyalty to institutions and organizations
  - Private
  - Dependable

- Boomers
  - Education
  - Independent
  - Fitness conscious
  - Question authority
  - Explore the inner world

- Generation X
  - "Neglected" by parents
  - Loyal to relationships
  - Serious about life
  - Stressed out, in counseling
  - Self-reliant
  - Skeptical

- Generation Y

  ◦ Cherished by parents (Decade of the Child)

  ◦ Groomed to achieve and excel

  ◦ Sense of entitlement

  ◦ Entrepreneurial hard workers

  ◦ Techo-savvy mediavores

  ◦ Socially conscious

  ◦ Full of self-esteem

  ◦ Spenders

CORE VALUES

- Traditionalists

  ◦ Dedication/sacrifice

  ◦ Conformity

  ◦ Law and order

  ◦ Patience

  ◦ Delayed reward

  ◦ Duty before pleasure

  ◦ Adherence to rules

- Boomers

  ◦ Optimism

  ◦ Team orientation

- Personal gratification
- Youth
- Health and Wellness
- Work

- Generation X
  - Diversity
  - Global thinking
  - Balance (work/home)
  - Techno-literacy
  - Fun
  - Informality

- Generation Y
  - Optimism
  - Civic Duty
  - Confidence
  - Street smarts
  - Sociability
  - Morality
  - Diversity

WHAT DO YOUNGER GENERATIONS WANT?

- Generation X
  - Responsibility
  - Travel
  - Movement
  - Advancement
  - Training and Education
  - Family friendly leave policies
  - Time off
  - Fun
- Generation Y
  - Entitlements
  - Time off
  - New equipment
  - New technology
  - Respect

WHAT ARE THE POSITIVES OFFERED BY YOUNGER GENERATIONS?

- Generation X
  - High energy

- ◦ Ethical
- ◦ Willing to question the system
- ◦ Expect accountability from management
- ◦ Technologically proficient
- ◦ Comfortable with change/Invite change

- Generation Y

  - ◦ Extremely technologically savvy
  - ◦ Street-smart/savvy
  - ◦ More accepting of other cultures, races, etc.
  - ◦ Resilient
  - ◦ Adept at multi-tasking
  - ◦ Experienced (deal with things at a much earlier age)

WHAT ARE THE NEGATIVES PRESENTED BY YOUNGER GENERATIONS?

- Generation X

  - ◦ Immediate gratification
  - ◦ Explanations (Why do we do it this way?)
  - ◦ Lack of work-ethic (perceived)
  - ◦ Unrealistic expectations
  - ◦ Want time off
  - ◦ No organizational loyalty

- Generation Y
  - Sense of entitlement
  - Short attention spans
  - Technologically dependent
  - Lack of work ethic (perceived)
  - Credit/spending problems
  - Want everything on their terms
  - Informal
  - Less responsible (not their fault)

LEADERSHIP CHALLENGES OF AN AGE DIVERSE WORKPLACE

- The 3 R's
  - Recruitment
  - Retention
  - Retirement
- Recruitment
  - How do we get them?
  - Utilize technology in recruitment
  - E-mail
  - Websites
  - Video

- ○ Re-evaluate job descriptions
- ○ What skills are we looking for?

- Retention

  - ○ How do we keep them?
  - ○ Motivate
  - ○ Challenge
  - ○ Educate

- Retirement

  - ○ How do we take care of them?

GENERATIONAL FRICTION: HOW TO ENCOURAGE OLDER AND YOUNGER WORKERS TO GET ALONG

- Strategies for Incorporating Generational Energy

  - ○ Recognize and accept a couple givens:
  - ○ This is inevitable. They are here and more are coming
  - ○ We (society) created these generations
  - ○ If you're a parent, it is your kids who are coming to work for you

- Use general characteristics as tools

  - ○ Motivation

- Provide recognition and appreciation

- Provide feedback

- Seek input

- Recognize expertise

- Offer incentives

  ◦ New assignments

  ◦ Varied assignments

  ◦ Time off

- Challenge

  ◦ Constantly increase and change demands

  ◦ Increase and improve standards

- Educate

  ◦ Formal training

  ◦ Informal education

  ◦ Open communication in your agency

INDEX

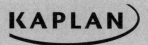

DATE DUE